This special edition of the *Van Alen Report* offers an exchange of information on how cities change after disaster, both by design, and sometimes, in spite of it. Since its inception in 1996, Van Alen Institute has been committed to the exchange of ideas, between cities, disciplines, design professionals and the community at large. After the attacks of September 11, this conviction deepened. Without information—not only the minute-to-minute updates of an emergency, but also the historical record of event and recovery that evolves into knowledge—cities can die, or return more misbegotten than reborn.

In 2001-2002, the Institute's trustees, members, and staff joined in an effort to acquire and disperse information, as well as offer interpretation grounded in experience. Often in partnership with other civic groups, projects ranged from posters, which used every available public surface to call for more thoughtfulness and less bluster, to mapping, interviewing, and briefing documents towards future memorials integrated with the life of the city. Carrying out initiatives underway before September 11, including a design competition and conference in Long Island City, Queens in fall 2001, and an urban design conference in spring 2002, underscored our vision of urban design's responsibility to learn from both the most local and the most global sources.

At the heart of this past year's work, exemplifying our convictions about the value and utility of urban knowledge, has been the Institute's "Renewing, Rebuilding, and Remembering" exhibit, installed from February through summer 2002. The exhibit's first message is that urban places, from very different cultures, do come back, even

renewing, rebuilding, remembering

after tolls in life and goods far more terrible than those of 9/11. Its concomitant message, in some cases more implicit than explicit in the exhibit, has been that there is much to learn, beyond the simple fact of renewal, from the seven cities in question.

Now, a year later, we have the opportunity to present the exhibit again, not only in its installation form at The Lighthouse, in Glasgow, Scotland, but also in this slim yet intense volume, with interviews and articles, as well as new images.

In the next year, our local, national, and international projects and partnerships are dedicated to one theme—understanding, articulating, and presenting new directions for public space, most prominently in a May 2003 exhibit and catalogue with major support from The Andy Warhol Foundation for the Visual Arts, and additional support from The Stephen A. and Diana L. Goldberg Foundation. Happily, we can learn not only from disaster and its aftermath, but also from many narratives of urban regeneration. In the exhibit and related programming, ranging from public forums and design competitions to the newly published *Beyond the Edge: New York's New Waterfront* (Princeton Architectural Press), we will strive to cut through the rhetoric of novelty to designs that renew public life, in vision and fact.

Raymond W. Gastil
Executive Director, Van Alen Institute

new york

2 Aerial view of Manhattan (2000) RWG / VAI

3

2001-03

SEPTEMBER 11, 8:46 a.m. American Flight 11 from Boston crashes into the North Tower at the World Trade Center.

9:03 a.m. United Flight 175 from Boston crashes into the South Tower at the WTC.
9:45 a.m. American Flight 77 crashes into The Pentagon.
10:05 a.m. The WTC South Tower collapses.
10:10 a.m. A large section of The Pentagon collapses.
10:10 a.m. United flight 93 crashes in a wooded area near Shanksville, Pennsylvania, after passengers confront hijackers.
10:28 a.m. The WTC North Tower collapses. 3

NOVEMBER 3 General Election, New York. Michael R. Bloomberg is Mayor-elect.

NOVEMBER 29 New York State and NYC name 16 board members (later increased to 21) of the Lower Manhattan Development Corporation (LMDC), a joint State-City initiative to oversee the rebuilding and revitalization of Lower Manhattan, defined as south of Houston Street.

DECEMBER 30 The first public viewing platform at Ground Zero opens at Church and Fulton streets.

JANUARY 17, 2002 *A New World Trade Center* exhibit opens at Max Protetch Gallery in NYC, the first broad overview of design approaches to the site.

FEBRUARY 1 New York New Visions, a coalition of 21 architecture, engineering, planning, landscape, and design organizations, formed in September 2001, releases *Principles for the Rebuilding of Lower Manhattan.*

FEBRUARY 12 *Renewing, Rebuilding, Remembering* exhibit opens at Van Alen Institute, the first exhibit to put New York's disaster in the context of other urban disasters in the past decade. 2 4

MARCH 11 "The Sphere" Interim Memorial is dedicated in The Battery, consisting of the recovered fragments of the steel and bronze sculpture by artist Fritz Koenig that had stood in the 5-acre WTC plaza.
   The temporary "Tribute in Light" is illuminated at 6:55 p.m. The memorial, situated within yards of Ground Zero in Battery Park City, consists of two banks of forty-four spotlights projecting into the night sky. 1

APRIL 9 The LMDC releases *Principles and*

Preliminary Blueprint for the Future of Lower Manhattan, which emphasizes the importance of transit, and connecting the site to downtown's historical monuments.

MAY 22 The LMDC and the Port Authority of New York and New Jersey, the bi-state entity that built the WTC and controls the 16-acre site, hire an urban design team to provide consulting services for an urban design and transportation planning study for the site.

MAY 30 An official ceremony ends the cleanup and recovery efforts at Ground Zero.

JUNE 10 *Imagine NY: The People's Visions* released, summarizing the 19,000 ideas for the site that came from over 230 meetings throughout the city and region, sponsored by a coalition initiated by the Municipal Art Society.

JULY 20 Nearly 5000 people gather at the Jacob K. Javits Center for the "Listening To The City" public meeting, led by the Regional Plan Association-organized Civic Alliance and America Speaks. Citizens exercise "direct democracy" regarding priorities for the site in response to six proposals released by the LMDC/ Port Authority. Participants are highly skeptical of the plans' merits. The Families Advisory Council of the LMDC presents its mission statement for the future memorial.

JULY 24 Exhibition of the WTC concept plans opens at Federal Hall on Wall Street.

AUGUST 12 Up to $4.55 billion is committed by the Federal government to revamp Lower Manhattan's infrastructure.

AUGUST 14 The LMDC issues a Request for Qualifications (RFQ) for five teams of architects and planners from around the world to take part in an October-November design process to prepare additional concept plans, and issues additional planning and design RFQs and contract extensions.

AUGUST 20 LMDC/PA initiate public hearings on permanent memorial ideas.

AUGUST 21 A viewing wall at Ground Zero is announced, following negative reactions to proposals to wrap the site in a 40-foot-high solid wall.

SEPTEMBER 11 Anniversary Ceremony at WTC site. First phase of WTC Viewing Wall completed.

2003 Expected completion of master plan, Spring. Expected selection of memorial design following international design competition, September.

retread or reinvention:
how cities change after disaster

The following transcript is from a round-table held at Van Alen Institute, New York, in August, 2002.

DIANA BALMORI Landscape and urban designer, Principal, Balmori Associates, and Chair, Temporary Memorials Committee, New York New Visions.

JOAN OCKMAN Director, Temple Hoyne Buell Center for the Study of American Architecture, Columbia University and organizer of "Out of Ground Zero: Case Studies in Urban Reinvention," a spring 2002 lecture series. Ockman edited the book by the same name published in fall 2002.

SHERIDA PAULSEN Architect and Chair, NYC Landmarks Preservation Commission.

LAWRENCE J. VALE Professor and Head, Department of Urban Studies and Planning and MacVicar Faculty fellow, Massachusetts Institute of Technology. Vale co-directed the spring 2002 colloquium "The Resilient City: Trauma, Recovery and Remembrance."

Raymond W. Gastil: The Buell Center and MIT had the same fundamental response to 9/11 that we did here—that there was something to learn from the experience of other cities after disaster. In the Institute's exhibit, we focused on the past decade, while at Columbia and MIT, your lecture series looked back further in history.

Joan Ockman: As a center operating within an academic institution, we felt we could contribute best by offering an historical and scholarly perspective on the situation downtown. Our approach was not so much to comfort people about how quickly cities bounce back in the aftermath of disasters as to explore a spectrum of responses. Indeed, some of the lectures we presented served as cautionary tales. But taken together, the nine cities we focused on, from the eighteenth century to the present, illustrated not just a set of variations on the theme of urban destruction but also demonstrated the multiple meanings and commonalities of urban experience.

Lawrence J. Vale: Many of us were taken aback by people saying "build bigger and stronger and better and show that terrorists can't win," rather than asking probing questions about what a trauma means at the societal level, let alone at the architectural or design level. We wanted to think much more holistically about what it means for a city to be subjected to a sudden traumatic disjuncture. Not only in what actually happens and the mechanics of recovery, but to see this as almost a diagnostic window into what the conditions were at that place at that time. We wanted to know who rebuilds what, where, and by what mechanisms. Our questions were both urbanistic ones, and also engaged what I call

the *design politics* of recovery. The term "Resilient City" does show an initial impulse to find reassurance or to help people come to terms with what had happened. As we progressed through the series, any lingering naïveté about that particular name dissipated. Just as it was clear that there had been remarkable forms of recovery, it was also very clear that there was also what Ed Linenthal calls "the toxic narrative" for many people involved in these events. If you think of these as moments that reveal key insights about society, you have a sense of what makes these things politically charged.

Diana Balmori: Some of that "charge" lies in the transformed and temporary site that such events leave behind. That site is a landscape of destruction. When the Federal Emergency Management Agency (FEMA) took charge of the WTC site, an informal network of people emerged who worked with GIS (Geographic Information Systems) and they produced 2,600 maps in six months showing us this constantly changing landscape. When we were launching the Temporary Memorials Committee and Laura Kurgan started the effort to do the "Around Ground Zero" map series, it was impossible to get the information from different parts of the city to do these maps—it was all locked up. The group GISMO (Geographic Information Systems Mapping Operations) and FEMA unlocked it in the case of Ground Zero. For those months, information really flowed.

These temporary landscapes of destruction and their documentation are important in such situations and they produce healing temporary responses be they Kobe's Paper Church, Beirut's Archaic Procession, or the Info-Box in Berlin, or even our own Temporary Memorials Committee's mapping effort.

LJV Yes, the struggle for memorial begins on the day, and it takes all sorts of forms. In the 1970s the National Science Foundation sponsored a research project called Reconstruction Following Disaster. They presented four phases: rescue, recovery, rebuilding, and then remembering. Yet whether you have a formal temporary memorials process, like the ones in New York, or not, memorializing begins at the start. There were all sorts of tensions over the temporary memorial process, not least of which involved the residents of Battery Park City, who didn't want to see themselves as part of "the site" or the landscape of remembrance.

JO I agree with Diana that the temporary or transitional developments downtown are significant and will, in retrospect, become key markers in the history of this crisis and this city. Time (and timing) is as important a dimension as space in the rebuilding process. Of course, one of the things that is extraordinary when an event like this occurs is that everything gets destabilized. Cities are full of petrified social structures and institutions, not to mention sedimented physical ones. In the wake of an event like this, everything momentarily seems to be opened up, to be up for grabs. Certain kinds of changes suddenly become imaginable. At the same time, how much really does or can change? One of the things I found interesting in the lecture in our series on New York, by Max Page, was his observation that after previous disasters befell New York—fires, epidemics, riots—not a whole lot was altered. Longer-term processes like waves of immigration, the rise of the automobile, and construction of commercial infrastructures (like the completion of the Erie Canal in 1825) have had far greater impact on the overall trajectory of the city. Of course, the events of September 11 are not quite like anything that has occurred before.

Disasters also sometimes have deferred or indirect effects. In Chicago after the fire of 1871, to take another example, there was a huge real-estate boom and a spate of shoddy building. This was followed a couple of years later by a national depression, when there was no building at all. As Ross Miller, our lecturer, pointed out, it was this post-fire experience rather than the disaster itself that ultimately engendered Chicago's great period of architectural modernism in the 1880s and 1890s. Architects like John Wellborn Root, Daniel Burnham, and Louis Sullivan were at a formative moment in their careers in the 1870s. It was the experience of living through this undistinguished period that inspired them to rebuild Chicago in a very different way.

LJV   We asked in our series whether we should assume that resilience is a good thing. Diane Davis wrote *Urban Leviathan* about 20th century Mexico City without saying very much about the 1985 earthquake. In her talk last spring, she said that she saw how the reverberations of that earthquake on the whole political system ultimately led to the downfall of the one-party state that had been in control for decades. The temporary, spontaneous actions by citizen groups revealed a lack of confidence in their government that people were eventually able to act upon. It is a telling moment to see who really wants "resilience" as a bounce back to where you were before, and who sees this as an opportunity to alter the status quo.

Sherida Paulsen: With all the constituencies involved in New York, we are at a temporary standstill. Nobody wants to go back to what was. They want something different, but they don't know what it is, and there are so many viewpoints that I think we're more in the Chicago model where we'll build something because we've got to build something. Right after 9/11, FEMA took charge, because they were the only ones who had a plan, and who had the resources and personnel. But today, we have a range of agendas set for the longer-term: New York New Visions came together, the Civic Alliance came together, and we have the Lower Manhattan Development Corporation, the Port Authority, the Mayor, and the Governor, all setting different agendas.

JO   Another interesting reflection that came out of the comparative perspective has to do with the role of individuals in the rebuilding process, and the presence or absence of creative urban thinkers at particular moments. Again, in Chicago, there was a vacuum after the fire; everybody rushed in but nobody had any big, significant ideas. In Lisbon, on the other hand, after

the earthquake of 1755 (an event that apparently would have registered 9.0 on the Richter scale!), the Marquis of Pombal emerged and took charge of the situation. He was a visionary, much like a Baron Haussman or a Robert Moses—and also a despot. As Kenneth Maxwell illustrated in a beautiful talk, Pombal turned Lisbon from a rather provincial and jumbled urban place into a commercial, Enlightenment-oriented city with modern sanitation and fireproofing systems. Two hundred and fifty years later the evidence of his intervention is still perfectly legible.

In the case of Hiroshima, you also had a significant individual. This time it was a young architect, Kenzo Tange, who appeared on the scene. Tange had an ambitious and visionary plan for reconstructing Hiroshima. Very little of it got realized beyond the central memorial complex, although he was allowed to return a decade later and implement a couple more components of his original scheme.

So today we have Bloomberg. It's interesting to think about how he and the other players on the scene right now will leave their mark.

RWG   There has been a call in New York that there should be cultural leaders convened to address the meaning and future of the site. Did this happen historically? Are "the best and the brightest" ever at the forefront of rebuilding?

JO   In Rotterdam, one of the other cities we looked at, something like this occurred. Rotterdam's reconstruction after World War II is often cited as an exemplary instance of rebuilding on a modernist model. You had enlightened members of the business community, progressive social thinkers, and modern architects putting their heads together. Many welcomed the opportunity to overhaul this antiquated and congested port city; in fact, they had wanted to do so for years before. Among other things, they saw Moses's highways in New York as an example to emulate. Yet the longer-term assessment of the postwar reconstruction has not been so positive, according to Han Meyer, a Dutch planner. By the 1960s, when postmodernism (exemplified by Rossi's theories of the city) was becoming ascendant in Europe, people in Rotterdam began to feel that the postwar planners and modernist ideology had done more damage to their city than the Nazi bombs. In recent decades the city has attempted in various ways to suture back the urban fabric and replan along more traditional Dutch or European lines.

LJV   Berlin is a place where the experts were called in as long as they fitted into the ideological preferences of East versus West—certainly in the 1950s experience of trying to come to terms with how to rebuild Berlin you had on the one hand the Stalinallee being proposed to highlight the palatial accommodation of the workers, and then the West's response with the Hansa Viertel, which brought in all the major figures in architecture and urbanism. The Germans have continued to emphasize competitions and exhibitions.

DB   Yet many American cities were affected by the destruction brought on in the 1960s not by war but by highways, which came in many cases accompanied by grand urban visions and transportation experts. New Haven had much of its center destroyed in this way and still hasn't recovered. It left the town with a fear of anything new. I was thinking that the building of highways in American cities has probably been as disastrous as earthquakes.

SP When you look at the World Trade Center, if the great achievement is that we can put back the old street pattern, this is really sad. The Trade Center was this great anomaly of modern design, sitting in the middle of itty-bitty streets, and it was done to allow commerce to continue to exist in Lower Manhattan, and now it is gone. At the Listening to the City event in July people responded strongly to the singular vision of the World Trade Center. Whether they liked the buildings or not, they felt that there was a singular vision, and that had been lost.

RWG In all of these programs, and for New York, the question comes up of how the tragic opportunity is seized upon to build a better city. Do we know what that is?

SP Who is this better city for? With competing interests between the tourist city and the local city and global city, is it possible to reconcile all these interests and give a piece to everybody?

DB What is this better city? The fundamental question may be not what, but how? Let me try to search for an answer: by making everything in it work the way natural processes work. How can we make the basic systems of a city like water or light work as in a natural process? Water, for example: we want to save it, clean it, we want it to reach rivers or groundwater slowly so it filters through soil and is cleaned and does not pollute or flood rivers. We want to retain it too, to return it to the atmosphere through the evapo-transpiration of plants, cooling the overheated atmosphere of the city in the process. How do we do that? We design surfaces to be absorbent. Does this mean all of Ground Zero is a park? No. How, then? By making building roofs into parks, by weaving parks into skyscrapers, by using green vertical walls, by paving streets with permeable materials. That's how. That's a place to start.

Let's take light: how can we make this part of the city the most beautifully lit environment in the world. Except for Times Square and a few of its tall buildings, New York has abominable lighting for its urban spaces. Can we think of it in terms of a system, not individual light fixtures, and can it be designed to use the energy of the sun through photovoltaics?

We start then with each of the basic systems that make up a city and ask how to have it work as closely as possible to a natural process. Which does not mean natural. You can get things to work as natural processes through mechanical means. Then see the consequences this has for buildings and their forms and design them at the end of this process, not the beginning. They need to be beautiful in the end, but their aesthetic is to be derived from the way we go about it, the how, which will deliver a city closer to living processes.

JO I agree. I think the ecological city is a key idea of our time. We're just waiting for the right architects, planners, and landscape designers to seize the initiative. The astonishingly far-reaching impact of 9/11 demon-strates that we can no longer afford to think about components of the city as piecemeal or independent conditions.

But may I go back to the example of Berlin for a moment? As part of our series we presented Berlin Babylon, a film by Hubertus Siegert completed in 2001. It's about the rebuilding of Berlin since the fall of the Wall. What's unusual about Siegert's approach is that rather than making a conventional documentary about the rebuilding program or a narrative of architectural achievements, he highlights, in a very poetic way, the brutality, banality, and arbitrariness of the urban process. The construction worker is a protagonist as much as the planner and the architect. The title of the film (which conflates Babel and Babylon) suggests the hubris of such a vast urban transformation.

DB I hope it doesn't happen that way in Lower Manhattan.

SP To start, we have to realize that any decision about the World Trade Center site has to be tied into a comprehensive public space idea for Lower Manhattan, and there has to be a program that captures the imagination for Lower Manhattan. I heard Senator Chuck Schumer describe his vision of putting the U.N. at Ground Zero at a recent breakfast. People were silent in this room: this great institution, and the location, and wouldn't this be great. Then he said the UN didn't want it, and offered his alternative, a great institute for the study of peace, and people in the room began talking while he was talking, unable to visualize that.

RWG Does the U.N. example show us that no one wants to be "centered," to have a headquarters, for fear of being a "target?" Is the idea of a center at risk?

JO Apart from practical and security concerns, there has certainly been a lot of talk at the theoretical level about decentering, about network cities, global cities, edge cities, polycentric cities as new urban paradigms in the twenty-first century, as opposed to the classic metropolis or empire city that New York was in the twentieth century. Obviously such a historical shift has major implications with respect to the way we think about rebuilding the World Trade Center site. Two speakers in our series argued very strenuously against giving up the idea of physical centrality and proximity that we have traditionally associated with the best spaces of public urban culture and democracy. One of them, Benjamin Barber, the author of the book *Jihad vs. McWorld,* warned against transforming cities into little more than privatized residential communities, shopping malls, and cybercafes on a kind of suburban model. The other, Milan Prodanovic, coming from the opposite world of Belgrade, offered the lesson of the way anti-cosmopolitan ideology and ethnic fundamentalism conspired to destroy Balkan cities, perpetrating another form of what he called "urbicide."

SP This goes into the question of what makes a city a city. I've heard phrases like "a bedroom community" being developed in Lower Manhattan, because, why would you need to build the office space back? That's a tragic thing to say about Lower Manhattan, because it is and has been all these things-commercial, industrial, and residential. It's been this amazing land of renewal happening for hundreds of years.

beirut

1 Phase 3 of Archaic Procession: Martyrs' Square (April 1998-December 1998)
NADIM KARAM

2 View of new housing developments from a destroyed building in Beirut Central District (November 1995)
CORINNA DEAN AND KLAUS WORSCHINGER / SOLIDERE

1   **Seaside Park**
       Phase 5 of Archaic Procession:
       June-December 1999

2   **Former Green Line**

3   **Starco**
       Phase 4 of Archaic Procession:
       April-June 1999

4   **Souks of Beirut**

5   **Al Omari Grand Mosque**

6   **Emir Mansour 'Assaf Mosque**

7   **Place de l'Etoile**
       SOLIDERE

8   **St. Elie Greek Catholic Church**

9   **St. Georges Greek Orthodox Church**

10   **Cardo Archaeological Site**
       Future Site of Garden of Forgiveness
       GUSTAFSON PORTER, LTD. (USA/UK)

11   **Martyrs' Square**
       Phase 3 of Archaic Procession:
       April-December 1998

12   **The Ring**
       Phase I of Archaic Procession:
       September-November 1997
       NADIM KARAM

13   **Beirut Central District with**
       United Nations House,
       center right
       SOLIDERE

14   **Riad el-Solh Square**
       Phase 2 of Archaic Procession:
       November 1997-March 1998

15   **St. Georges Maronite Cathedral**

16   **Saifi Village**

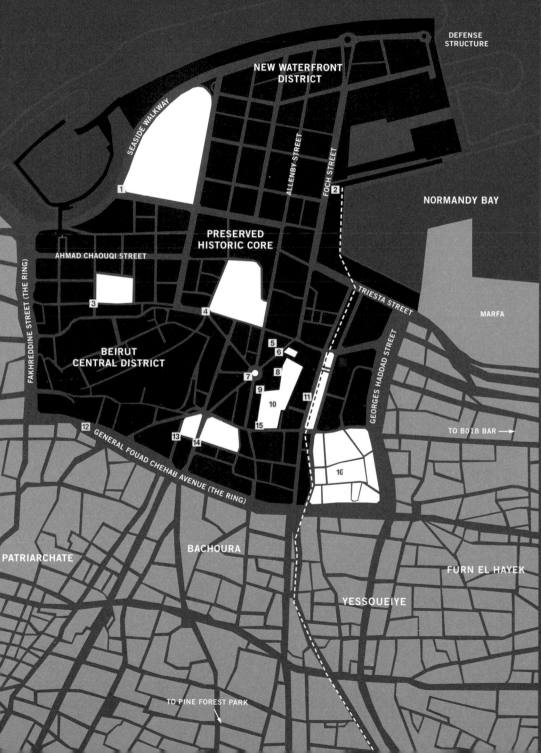

1/4 MILE

N

MEDITERRANEAN SEA

NEW WATERFRONT DISTRICT

DEFENSE STRUCTURE

SEASIDE WALKWAY

ALLENBY STREET

FOCH STREET

1

2

NORMANDY BAY

PRESERVED HISTORIC CORE

AHMAD CHAOUQI STREET

TRIESTA STREET

MARFA

3

4

FAKHREDDINE STREET (THE RING)

BEIRUT CENTRAL DISTRICT

GEORGES HADDAD STREET

5

6

7

8

9

10

11

15

TO B018 BAR →

12

13

14

16

GENERAL FOUAD CHEHAB AVENUE (THE RING)

PATRIARCHATE

BACHOURA

FURN EL HAYEK

YESSOUEIYE

TO PINE FOREST PARK

beirut

During the seventeen years of civil war in Lebanon (1975-1992), Beirut became a divided city. The 1.5 million inhabitants of various ethnic and religious denominations were entrenched in distinct urban districts and a "Green Line" was drawn between the eastern and western parts of the city, separating its Christian and Muslim inhabitants. The fighting had caused so much damage that by the end of the war in 1992 the city center was practically erased. In 1994 Prime Minister Hariri founded SOLIDERE, a company to over-see the reconstruction of the Beirut Central District and restore basic services to this devastated city. The master plan, by architects and urban planners Dar Al-Handasah (Shair & Partners), was presented by SOLIDERE in 1997, and proposed the development of 15 million square feet of commercial and residential space, an arts complex, and several public parks and shopping amenities as well as a memorial, a proposal made to SOLIDERE by Beirut's citizens. The hadîquat as-Samâb (Garden of Forgiveness), being designed by landscape architect Kathryn Gustafson of Gustafson Porter, Ltd. (USA/UK), transforms the 6 acre site of the former Roman road, the Cardo Maximus, situated next to St. Georges Maronite Church, into a public garden while at the same time protecting the archaeological remains.

Prior to rebuilding, artist Nadim Karam conceived of "Archaic Procession," a public art project installed in 1997 along the periphery of the ruined buildings in downtown Beirut. His objective was to break up the war-torn environment with sculptures that would signal future reconstruction and innovation in the city. Twenty sixteen-foot tall steel sculptures, abstract forms of the human body, that were lit at night, were displayed in five distinct neighborhoods over two years. "The simplicity of the silhouettes against devastated and ruined buildings transformed the site into a stage upon which the citizens felt they could celebrate their daily lives, escaping for a moment from routine and anxiety," explains Karam.

timeline> 1975-77

SUMMER Civil war breaks out between the Muslim coalition allied with Palestinian groups and the Christian-dominated militias.

1975-1976 The "Green Line" (a term borrowed from Israeli military mapping vocabulary and referring to a strip of trees and grass that grows in and around buildings and streets in no man's land) is drawn to segregate the main opposing militias.

Beirut city center is part of the demarcation line and is closed off and its civilian population forced out. Office buildings are used as military bases. Replacement locations for businesses are found in residential areas in the suburbs of Beirut.

APRIL 1976 Syrian military forces impose a cease-fire at the request of the Lebanese president, Suleiman Franjieh, and with the approval of the Arab League of States.

1977 The Lebanese Ministry of Planning is replaced with the Council for Development and

4

Reconstruction (CDR). Beirut's reconstruction becomes a priority.

1978-83

Sporadic violence continues. Israeli troops enter southern Lebanon to eliminate Palestinian bases.

Residents and businesses are forced to move to the periphery of the city center as fighting continues in Beirut and the suburbs.

Public infrastructure, residential and historic buildings—such as the 17th century Emir Mansour 'Assaf Mosque—and factories are damaged. Buildings are bulldozed to accommodate military hardware and heliports.

1982 United Nations peacekeeping forces are sent into the area. Israeli forces withdraw, leading to a temporary break in fighting. Three months later Israeli forces return.

AUGUST 23 The Lebanese parliament elects Bashir Gemayel President of the Lebanese Republic.

SEPTEMBER 14 Bashir Gemayel is killed in the explosion of the Kataeb party headquarters.

The geography of the city radically changes due to destruction and rebuilding. The demography of the city's population, its social structure and economic networks are also affected. The east-west divide affects the commercial and transportation networks: bus lines stop at the demarcation line, roads are closed, and only a few gates are kept open. Distinct territories emerge with their own particular geographical identity.

OCTOBER 23, 1983, 6:22 a.m. A suicide bomber kills 300 U.S. and French troops. Western forces pull out of Beirut.

1988-94

A parliamentary power struggle leads to the formation of rival Christian and Muslim governments.

1989 The Lebanese parliament accepts a peace accord for national reconciliation. Maronite Rene Mooed is elected as President, but is assassinated two weeks later.

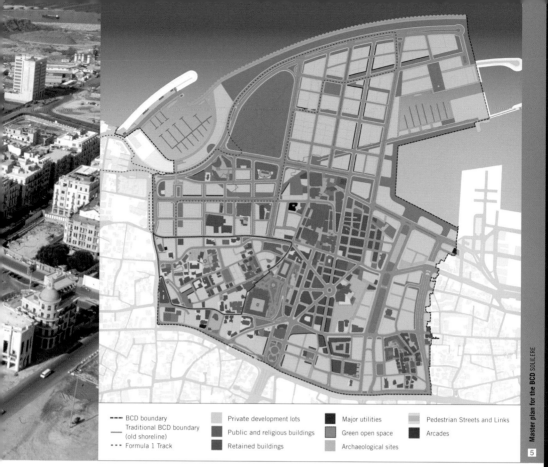

--- BCD boundary
— Traditional BCD boundary (old shoreline)
--- Formula 1 Track

Private development lots
Public and religious buildings
Retained buildings

Major utilities
Green open space
Archaeological sites

Pedestrian Streets and Links
Arcades

5

1991 The Council for Development and Reconstruction (CDR) commissions the architecture and urban planning firm, Dar Al-Handasah (Shair & Partners) to develop a master plan for the city. **3**

1992 The civil war officially ends.

OCTOBER 22 Rafiq Hariri becomes Prime Minister of Lebanon. Hariri and Lebanese President Elias Hrawi set out to stabilize the Lebanese economy and rebuild Beirut's infrastructure.

SPRING 1993 Dar Al-Handasah (Shair & Partners) organizes a number of public seminars for citizens to comment on the master plan.

NOVEMBER CDR launches an international design ideas competition for redevelopment of the former marketplace, the "Souks of Beirut," into a 328,000 square foot retail, office, entertainment and cultural district.

MAY 5, 1994 The master plan is approved. Prime Minister Hariri founds SOLIDERE,

> **"The master plan is invoking a new, contemporary model for a city center—not just business and government but, more importantly, a lively residential and multi-functional heart to a city, with recreation, entertainment, shopping and cultural uses for all."**
>
> **Angus Gavin,** Manager, Urban Development Division, SOLIDERE

the Lebanese Company for the Development and Reconstruction of Beirut Central District (BCD) to implement the master plan for the approximately 6 million square foot area. Immediate plans include restoring all infrastructure, working out property rights involving owners, tenants and lease-holders, supplying provisions for squatters who have occupied the area during and following the war, and addressing the environmental problems of the garbage dump that formed on an artificial island jutting into the Normandy Bay, north of the BCD. **5**

JULY 16 Drisin, McFarlane; Annabel Karim & Valode & Pistre; and Mark Saade & Associates are named winners of the competition for the Souks. Subsequently, SOLIDERE commissions architect and planner Jad Tabet to undertake a detailed master plan for the Souks, incorporating many of the best ideas in the competition. Subsequently, six teams are appointed to carry out the architectural design now under construction: Rafael Moneo (Spain), Jad Tabet (Lebanon), Kevin Dash (U.K.), Valode & Pistre (France), Nabil Tabbara (Lebanon) and Olivier Vidal (France).

SEPTEMBER 17 An open-air concert in Martyrs' Square by the Lebanese singer Feyrouz inaugurates the Beirut Reconstruction Project.

1997-99

Oussama Kabbani, SOLIDERE's Manager of Town Planning, presents the revised master plan for BCD. The project includes: the reconstruction and development of 15 million square feet of financial and office buildings, commercial centers, hotels, centers for the arts, public parks and recreational areas on the sea with gardens and tree-lined promenades extending along Beirut's coastal Boulevard.

The new reconstruction process consists of a two-phased plan:

- Phase One includes all infrastructure and restoration in the traditional BCD. New projects will include the "Souks of Beirut," "Saifi Village," a residential complex, and administrative buildings such as the United Nations House. **2**

- Phase Two will continue the development of the traditional BCD, finalize residential developments

in "Wadi Abou jamil" and focus on the areas surrounding Martyrs' Square and United Nations Plaza and construction of the marina at the eastern edge of the waterfront. **7 9**

SEPTEMBER The "Archaic Procession," a collection of 16-foot high steel metal statues by Lebanese artist Nadim Karam, is installed on the periphery of the BCD on the elevated highway, The Ring. The installation is the first in a five-phase public art project that will run until December 1999. The first installation on The Ring runs until November 1997.

OCTOBER The Grand Theatre, built in the 1930s and damaged in the war, reopens for performances while undergoing reconstruction.

NOVEMBER "Archaic Procession" moves to Ryadh el-Solh Square where it will remain on view until March 1998. **6**

FEBRUARY 1998 Dedication of the United Nations House by UN Secretary General Kofi Annan.

APRIL 18 B018, a bar and restaurant owned by Naji Gebrane, opens at "La Quarantaine" lot #317. The bar is built on the former site of the city harbor's quarantine station, which in 1939 was transformed

Martyrs' Square under construction with Martyrs' Statue at left (November 1995) CORINNA DEAN AND KLAUS WURSCHINGER / SOLIDERE [7]

BO18 bar on the former site of the city harbor's quarantine station BERNARD KHOURY ARCHITECTS [8]

Sign showing a rendering of new promenade from Martyrs' Square to the waterfront SOLIDERE [9]

into a refugee camp for Armenians fleeing Turkish persecution and in 1975 housed approximately 20,000 Palestinian, Kurdish and Lebanese refugees. The main feature of the 40 x 60 foot underground bar is the roof, which slides open on pistons. [8]

"Archaic Procession" moves to Martyrs' Square where it will remain on view until December 1998. [1]

NOVEMBER 24 Army Commander Emile Lahoud is sworn in as the 11th Lebanese President.

DECEMBER 3 Mr. Salim Hoss becomes Lebanon's new Prime Minister following Hariri's resignation.

1999 French architect and planner, Michael Macary works with SOLIDERE to designate a 77,000 square foot area just below street level in the Cardo archaeological site (through which the Green Line originally ran), for a "Garden of Forgiveness." The site is surrounded by some of Lebanon's most important churches and mosques. [4]

APRIL "Archaic Procession" moves to the Starco area where it will remain on view until June 1999.

> "The continuous movement of the "Archaic Procession" in downtown Beirut was reminiscent of the provisional aspect of the city as a whole. Along with the emptiness around, it became a justification to rethink the city in terms of a cultural void instead of a real estate one."
>
> **Makram El-Kadi,** Architect

JUNE "Archaic Procession" moves to the Seaside Walkway where it will remain on view until December 1999.

AUGUST 4 An international design competition for the "Garden of Forgiveness" is announced. Six designers are invited to submit designs. The design is to meet four main objectives: assist the post-war reconciliation in Lebanon, help recreate the heart of the city with public spaces open to all citizens, respect Beirut's archaeological heritage, and contribute to a new sense of common heritage and identity for the future of Lebanon.

NOVEMBER SOLIDERE commissions Skidmore, Owings & Merrill to develop a detailed master plan for the new Waterfront District, which will include a Monaco-style Grand Prix racing track.

MARCH 20 Kathryn Gustafson of Gustafson Porter, Ltd. (USA/UK) is announced the winner of

10

11

12

the competition for the "Garden of Forgiveness." Her design is based on three conceptual principles: history, the present and future, and timelessness. References to the three dimensions are implied throughout the garden: A stone table becomes a metaphor for a meeting place. Planting becomes a series of metaphors—the cedar denoting the ancient forest, the palm denoting the coast. Various terraces reflect the typical agricultural landscape, contained within a stone and rock gorge with a water channel flowing through—representing the possibility of life. **10 11 12**

OCTOBER Rafiq Hariri (for the second time) becomes Prime Minister of Lebanon.

JUNE 2001 Inauguration of the restored 16th century Emir Mansour 'Assaf Mosque.

SUMMER Construction of the "Saifi Village" residential complex is completed.

SUMMER 2002 Aspects of the Waterfront District, built on a one-mile stretch of reclaimed land, are completed, including two marinas, a seaside promenade and drive, a 236,000 square foot public park and BIEL, the Beirut International Exhibition and Leisure Center.

2004 Scheduled completion of Phase 2 of the reconstruction efforts in the Central Business District.

SUMMER Expected completion of the "Souks of Beirut."

AUTUMN Expected completion date of the "Garden of Forgiveness."

2023

Scheduled completion of the Waterfront District.

Beirut Central District Master Plan:
DEVELOPER: SOLIDERE
Angus Gavin, Division Manager, Urban Development Division
Oussama Kabbani, former Town Planning Manager

Archaic Procession:
CLIENT: Societé Generale de Banque au Liban, SOLIDERE
ARTIST: Nadim Karam, Principal, Atelier Hapsitus
LIGHTING DESIGNER: Debbas

Garden of Forgiveness:
CLIENT: SOLIDERE
LANDSCAPE ARCHITECTS: Gustafson Porter, Ltd. (USA/UK)
ENGINEERS: Ove Arup & Partners
ARCHAEOLOGIST: Richard Hughes
QUANTITY SURVEYORS: Northcrofts

master-planning

ANGUS GAVIN and NADIM KARAM
in conversation with Zoë Ryan

Gavin is Manager of the Urban Development Division of SOLIDERE, Beirut. From 1992-3 he worked as a consultant for Dar Al-Handasah (Shair & Partners) as Head of the Planning Team responsible for developing a master plan for the city. Karam is Dean of the Faculty of Architecture, Art and Design, Notre Dame University, Beirut, and Principal of Atelier Hapsitus, an interdisciplinary public art and architecture firm.

Zoë Ryan: Angus - Is the Beirut Central District (BCD) still considered the dominant center of the metropolitan region? How is its reconstruction and renewal seen as assisting in the postwar reconciliation of the city?

Angus Gavin: Beirut matches quite closely the "poly-nuclear" structure of most modern cities, so the BCD is the focus, in a hierarchy with other centers. Lebanon's war caused massive population dispersal and polarization of the city into sectarian enclaves. Historically central Beirut has always represented multi-cultural Lebanon's "common ground." Its re-establishment is an implicit objective of the master plan, being implemented in three ways: to recreate Beirut's "meeting point" by making the pedestrian Conservation Area the focal point of the city; to create public spaces with 457 acres of green space; and to integrate archaeological sites and historic buildings and create a national cultural life downtown.

ZR Angus - In 1991, an unprecedented law was passed in Beirut allowing the establishment of a private sector real estate company, SOLIDERE, rather than a centralized government agency or a development corporation, to control the reconstruction of the BCD. What was the strategy behind this decision? How is SOLIDERE operated and managed?

AG The legislation had been developed during the war years. The essential principle was to use the government's powers of eminent domain to pool existing owners' property rights together with new investors by forming a joint stock company in which previous owners remained the controlling shareholders. Lebanon's immediate postwar government extended the existing legislation to apply to development of the entire city center in accordance with a master plan. The SOLIDERE model is, however, unique to Beirut and grew out of the situation at the close of the war: weakened public institutions incapable of undertaking such large-scale urban development; limited government resources; and extensive war damage in the capital's downtown.

ZR Angus - Over 30 public seminars were held for citizens to give feedback on the preliminary master plans developed by the consultants Dar Al-Handasah (Shair & Partners). How was this process organized?

AG In Lebanon there are, as yet, no mandated public inquiry or consultation procedures built into the planning process, as in the West. Nevertheless, the planners Dar Al-Handasah were asked to organize a series of public presentations. Public debate and a critique of the plan by a group of professionals were fundamental to the development of a new master plan.

ZR During the planning stages their was much criticism of the master plan, which included it was too monumental and did not preserve enough of the memory of Beirut. What kind of city center is now being visualized? (Among the critiques of the master plan before its completion and implementation are: "The Reconstruction of Beirut: A Lost Opportunity," by Assem Salaam, *AA Files*, Summer, 1994 and "Beirut between Past and Future," by Saree Makdisi, *ANY*, March/April 1994.)

AG The problem was that the master plan was made by architects, not urban designers or planners. This was reflected in its concern for three-dimensional architectural form that seemed precise and predetermined. The new plan is more sensitive to existing context. Changes include doubling the number of heritage buildings, recognizing and integrating historical layers, and connecting the center to its surroundings. And finally the master plan is seen not as a fixed plan, but a flexible planning framework.

Nadim Karam: Although it seems that all redevelopment has been set in planning terms, the city is still a big empty canvas where visionaries can and should propose their own visions.

ZR Angus - Is it still true today that the main objective of the revised master plan developed in 1994 is to create a city center that is more than a central business district but is 24 hours and mixed-use?

AG Yes, although we must not overlook two other goals: to re-create the "common ground" and create a pole of quality and excellence that will help reestablish the city's international role. What we are doing in central Beirut is developing a new form of city center—active, live-in, multi-functional, defined more accurately as a Central Area. Our conviction is that if we wire this Central Area with high-speed networks and sophisticated telematics as is planned, we can create an almost irresistible attraction.

ZR Angus - Discrete areas of the city, such as the Souks, are being developed based on concepts from international design ideas competitions. Why are competitions important? Have others been part of the planning process?

AG Design competitions and the pursuit of design excellence are important aspects of city making. You will not reposition Beirut, after all the disasters and setbacks that it has endured, without applying world class design talent. The Souks, now half constructed, was the subject of an open, international design competition. Such competitions are time-consuming and costly. They attract large numbers of entries—over 350 in the case of the Souks—which means it is often difficult to entice leading designers to enter. I believe, however, that special circumstances apply in the case of Martyrs' Square. We are currently preparing an open ideas competition for this area. In general, we make greater use of limited competitions as a means of securing high quality design. The Garden of Forgiveness and Beirut Marina were the subject of such competitions.

ZR How do you animate public spaces that have as difficult a history as Beirut's?

AG There is no doubt that public art has a role here, to give meaning and symbolism to public space. Beirut's celebrated Martyrs' Square statue—now restored with its bullet holes—resides in the collective memory, but still has to take its place in the square. Beirut as a whole is in such short supply of green spaces that almost any provision will create a needed attraction. The question, then, is can these spaces be mobilized as a "social arena" for reconciliation? My view is that we need to provide public space for recreational use, not only for local residents and users but also for the relatively deprived residents of some of the districts immediately adjacent to the city center to reinforce the idea of the center as the meeting point for all.

NK Beirut is a city that has been rebuilt several times, and new reconstruction is simply another layer that is built on top of existing ruins. I am not saying that we need to forget the old Beirut, and what happened to it, but I do think that we are building another urban strata in Beirut's history, and animating the public spaces in a way that is a reflection of our contemporary Lebanese culture.

ZR Nadim - What was your inspiration for the Archaic Procession— a series of sculptures that were installed in the BCD between 1997-99?

NK There was a need for emancipation in different zones within the city through ephemeral, accumulated actions that tried to break through the existing network and agitate its very structure.

ZR How did the Archaic Procession come about?

NK In the tense postwar climate it was impossible for authorities to decide on one artist from whatever religion to "represent" downtown revival—my project worked because it was temporary. It did cause some polemics but these usually abated when the sculptures changed location. I wanted to draw people's attention to the destroyed city center in an abstract and oblique way. I tried as much as possible to shift the sculptures overnight, so that people woke up one day to find that the sculptures they saw on the bridge the previous evening were missing, but rediscovered them on the roofs of buildings.

AG One of the engaging aspects of Nadim's Procession was that it surprised us, appearing one day on the edge of the highway that links east and west Beirut, then high up on the top of disfigured buildings. It shook our perceptions of the devastated city with a somewhat irreverent sense of child-like fun. Life, it seemed, was just around the corner and about to return.

ZR Have artists, or have you Nadim, been involved in the design and planning process of the Beirut Central District?

AG Artists have not been directly involved in the planning process. However, in addition to Nadim's temporary Procession, we have commissioned works from several Lebanese sculptors including two pieces by Selwa Choucair, and planned, with them, where to site the works within the landscape design of various public spaces. We have also just completed a sculpture garden, where we intend to hold revolving exhibitions.

NK A few months ago, I was invited by SOLIDERE to participate in a closed architectural competition for the Beirut Marina. In this project, we were mainly concerned by the complexity of the forces on and around the site. Unfortunately, there was no winner.

ZR Has culture been an important driver for renewal and revitalization in Beirut?

AG Culturally led regeneration has recently become one of the favored strategies for inner city renewal. Successful examples are Glasgow, Dublin's Temple Bar, Bilbao, and Barcelona. Beirut's rich cultural heritage has influenced our development strategy. As well as communicating Beirut's history, we want to create a major cultural focus downtown and have a wish list of projects pending funding.

NK Culture should be an important driving force for the renewal and revitalization of Beirut. We are still far from reaching a healthy balance between the commercial and the cultural, although much effort has been made until now.

ZR Angus - Please explain the history behind the Garden of Forgiveness and its future site on the Cardo archaeological site. Was it conceived of as a memorial?

AG Four years ago SOLIDERE was approached by Alexandra Asseily, a professional psychotherapist, with the concept. She felt that a space for reflection and healing was essential to enable Lebanon to exorcise its recent past. The Chairman was profoundly impressed by the idea and after studying various options we identified a site close to the wartime Green Line. A limited international design competition was prepared. In 2000, a design was chosen but lengthy procedures were necessary to amend the master plan and obtain the support of the Director General of Antiquities. The deciding event that actually encouraged us to move ahead with the project was the September 11th disaster in the United States. The idea touches raw nerves here. Some believe they have no need to forgive, or be forgiven, and have raised objections to the name. This is not about memories of lost loved ones, but about a difficult process for all those who survived. In August 1999, Nasser Chammaa, the competition's Chairman wrote: "The project...must assist the process of postwar reconciliation and healing in Lebanon...[and] must contribute to a new sense of common heritage, identity and spirit of the future for all the Lebanese communities."

ZR Angus - Please describe the winning design by Kathryn Gustafson and how it fulfilled the brief the best.

AG The choice, essentially, revolved around two main issues: how to capture the theme of forgiveness, and how to integrate the archaeology. Some of the other designs treated the theme of forgiveness with perhaps too obvious, if heartfelt symbolism. This sits uneasily with Lebanese sensitivities. Instead, Kathryn proposed a garden that symbolizes, not lessons of reconciliation, but a spirit of regained unity, expressed by bringing together elements of Lebanon's unique landscapes. Kathryn's winning design presented archaeological features integrated within the landscape. Perversely to some, the concept required the backfilling and covering up of significant areas of the ruins. However, the archaeologist on the jury defended this as accepted good conservation practice.

1   The Brandenburg Gate enclosed by the Berlin Wall in the Soviet-occupied sector of East Berlin (1961) ASSOCIATED PRESS

2   Info-Box © JÜRG HEMPEL, GERMANY

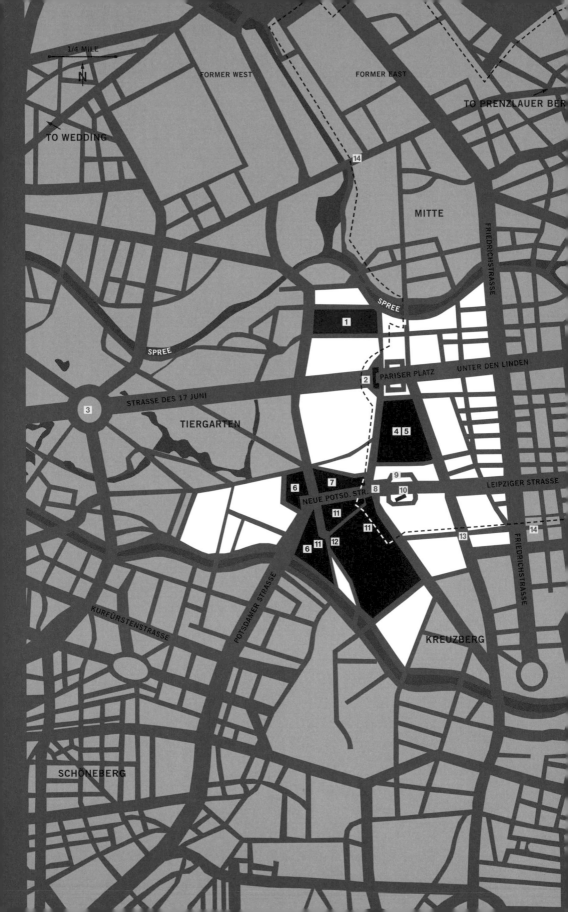

1   **Reichstag**

2   **Brandenburg Gate**

3   **Siegessäule (Victory Column)**

4   **Future Site of the Memorial to the Murdered Jews of Europe**
EISENMAN ARCHITECTS

5   **Model of the Memorial for the Murdered Jews of Europe**
EISENMAN ARCHITECTS

6   **Kulturforum**

7   **Sony Center**

8   **Potsdamer Platz**
DENANCÉ MICHEL
© RENZO PIANO BUILDING WORKSHOP

9   **Leipziger Platz**

10   **Info-Box**
© JÖRG HEMPEL, GERMANY

11   **DaimlerChrysler**

12   **Marlene Dietrich Platz**

13   **Former Berlin Wall**

14   **Former Checkpoint Charlie**

berlin

Berlin, the center of so much of Europe's cultural, artistic and intellectual production in the early twentieth century, had, under the National Socialist regime also become the symbolic capital of hatred, genocide and Fascism. Allied bombing destroyed sixty percent of the city by the end of the war, turning most of the urban fabric into rubble. In 1961 the government of communist East Germany built a wall around West Berlin to stop East Germans from using it as a departure gate to the West and for thirty years the Berlin Wall stood as an icon of the policies of the Cold War. Its removal after the reunification of Germany was both a cause for celebration and a reminder of the scars left by the Second World War. The former site of the wall, the adjacent plazas Potsdamer and Leipziger Platz, was before the war the transportation and commercial hub of Berlin. When the Wall fell, civic and business leaders seized the opportunity to reconnect the city and create an international commercial center for the burgeoning capital that today has 3.5 million inhabitants. When, in 1992, Daimler-Benz (now DaimlerChrysler) picked Renzo Piano and Christoph Kohlbecker's master plan as the winner of the international architectural competition to design their 18.5 acre-portion of the entire 118.6 acre site (master planned by Heinz Hilmer and Christoph Sattler) this vision began to crystallize.

In 1994 Schneider + Schumacher Architekten's design for the Info-Box was chosen to contain a temporary facility to explain the process of construction at Potsdamer Platz. After learning about the planning process in the galleries, one could see the realization of the new construction throughout the site from the rooftop viewing platform. At the same time, to address the heavy history of this war-torn city and its position as the former capital of the Third Reich, a series of design competitions were organized for a Memorial for the Murdered Jews of Europe. In 1999 Peter Eisenman and Richard Serra's proposal for a grid of 4,000 concrete columns measuring up to 13 feet in height was chosen as the winner. After much discussion and subsequent alterations to the original design and program, including reducing the number of columns, incorporating a study center, and Serra's subsequent resignation from the project, it is currently under construction and is to be completed in 2004.

timeline> 1939-45

The bombing of World War II destroys approximately 60 percent of the city. Berlin's population is reduced to approximately 2.8 million from a pre-war high of 4.4 million.

Following the defeat of the Nazi regime in World War II (1939-1945), the victorious Allied Powers—the United States, Britain, France, and the Union of Soviet Socialist Republics (USSR)—divide Germany into four zones, each occupied by one of the Allied Powers. They also divide Berlin, which was in the Soviet sector, into similar zones. The Soviet-controlled sector of the city becomes known as East Berlin, and the Western-occupied sector becomes known as West Berlin.

1945-60

1940s and 1950s As Berlin becomes a focus of the Cold War, West Berlin's Allied protectors strive to keep the city alive by providing massive economic assistance. During the Cold War years, West Berlin rebuilds its infrastructure and residential areas,

Daimler-Benz Project for Potsdamer Platz
Renzo Piano/Christoph Kohlbecker

■ Restaurant/Café	■ Cinema
■ Housing	■ Kindergarden
■ Theater	■ Hotel
■ Offices	■ Cinema
■ Shopping	■ Vertical Circulation

5

expands its subway system, and constructs a major international airport. A new central business district is developed southwest of Tiergarten along the Kurfürstendamm and other nearby streets.

JUNE 24, 1948 Joseph Stalin halts all traffic in and out of the Russian sector of Berlin in Marienborn. Food is airlifted into the area.

SEPTEMBER 30, 1949 Soviets reopen land and water routes into Berlin and the airlift is phased out.

NOVEMBER The USSR establishes a separate administration in East Berlin, which becomes the capital of the German Democratic Republic (East Germany) while Bonn becomes the capital of West Germany.

JUNE 1953 Public dissatisfaction with conditions in East Berlin erupts in demonstrations that quickly spread to the rest of East Germany.

1961

Approximately 2.7 million people leave East Germany by way of West Berlin.

AUGUST 13 In order to stop the outward flow of its citizens, East Germany unexpectedly constructs a fortified wall around West Berlin. All roads come to a dead end at the wall (except for a few heavily guarded border crossings). The subway system is rerouted into two separate systems. During the period between 1961 and 1989, at least 80 East Germans are killed trying to cross over the wall into the West. The areas on either side of the wall become partially abandoned. ■

1989

NOVEMBER 9 A government spokesman announces during an East German evening news broadcast that the Berlin Wall is open. Citizens rally around the wall and tear down large sections.

1990

FEBRUARY-JUNE The East and West German governments and the wartime Allies agree to a plan for unification in what is known as the Two-Plus-Four talks.

6

OCTOBER 3 East and West Germany are officially united. The German government decides to gradually move the federal government from Bonn to Berlin, precipitating a building boom in the city.

1991

The Government announces an international design competition for the city center, "Ideenwettbewerb Potsdamer/Leipziger Platz," and invites 16 architectural firms to contribute urban planning concepts. **3**

OCTOBER 1 Architects Heinz Hilmer and Christoph Sattler's design wins. Their scheme seeks to revitalize the area through a mixture of commercial, residential and entertainment facilities and by reestablishing the site's historic street plan. Their design becomes the basis for a set of guidelines to develop approximately 1 million square foot surrounding Potsdamer Platz and Leipziger Platz.

1992

> **"The last time I was in Marlene Dietrich Platz it was a hot summer's night, a school class came out of the cinema and all stripped off and jumped into the water basin! Not strictly allowed, but to me that speaks deeply about the good feeling they had about the place."**
>
> **Herbert Dreiseitl,** Atelier Dreiseitl

Daimler-Benz AG (now DaimlerChrysler) who since 1989 had owned a portion of the site, announces their own architectural competition and invites 14 firms to develop proposals for the 18.5 acre site. The goal of the competition is to create a site that links the Kulturforum, an area of museums and galleries planned in the 1960s by Hans Scharoun, to the west and the new commercial area on Leipziger Platz to the east, following the design guidelines outlined in the winning proposal by Hilmer & Sattler.

Renzo Piano and Christoph Kohlbecker are announced the winners of the Daimler competition. Their scheme divides the area into 19 individual construction sites centered around the new Marlene Dietrich Platz, with different architects commissioned for each site. Building projects around the site include: IMAX Cinema (1998) by Piano and Kohlbecker; office and commercial buildings on Linkstraße (1998) by Richard Rogers Partnership, Steffen Lehmann & Partner + Arata Isozaki & Associates; the Mercedes-Benz Headquarters (1998) by Jose Rafael Moneo and the Sony Center (2000) by Helmut Jahn of

7

8

Murphy/Jahn Architects. The Sony Center, in particular, provokes debate. The commercial, mall-like features of the building (a large, semi-enclosed courtyard) present a new type of urban design in Berlin. Concerns are raised about the building's inward orientation. Public art pieces by Keith Haring, Jeff Koons, Robert Rauschenberg and Mark di Suvero are installed in the Daimler-Benz headquarters. **4 7**

Atelier Dreiseitl, a firm based in Ueberlingen, Germany and specializing in urban hydrology and water works is invited to design a water system for Marlene Dietrich Platz. Atelier Dreiseitl's project has multiple functions, both as a water feature within the Platz but also as a useful way of recycling rainwater that collects in underground tanks beneath the buildings. **8 9**

A competition for a Memorial for the Murdered Jews of Europe is announced. 528 submissions are received for the 204,500 square foot site, once part of the no-man's land along the Berlin Wall and now located between the new Potsdamer Platz and the Brandenburg Gate.

> "Four weeks after the Info-Box was opened, the public demand for access to the roof was so overwhelming that we were asked to finally add a platform on the top. I could imagine a similar box at the World Trade Center, but more as a site for discussions and as a forum for the exchange of ideas."
>
> **Kristin Dirschl,** Architect
> Schneider + Schumacher Architekten

1994-95

SUMMER The Berlin City Administration asks investors engaged in construction on Potsdamer Platz to organize an invited design competition for a temporary Info-Box. To be built at Leipziger Platz, the goal is to find a design for an information pavilion where investors can present their plans for rebuilding and explain the construction process. The Info-Box will also act as a viewing platform overlooking Potsdamer Platz.

DECEMBER Out of the five proposals Schneider + Schumacher Architekten's design is announced the winner and construction begins soon after. Made from steel panels typically used by contractors to make the containers prevalent on building sites, the 50 x 200 foot box will be built on Leipziger Platz at an estimated cost of $4.8 million. Painted bright red and suspended 21 feet above ground on stilts, the box will be instantly visible amidst the chaotic background of the building site that will be the newly rebuilt Potsdamer Platz.

The interior of the building is divided into two main areas around a three-story entrance hall. The area facing the Potsdamer Platz construction site contains the general-purpose rooms; on the first floor, there is a souvenir shop; above this is a conference room; and on the top floor there is a café with views over the construction site. On the other side of the building are exhibition areas, extending over the three stories, and public amenities.

> "The enormity and scale of the horror is such that any attempt to represent it by traditional means is inevitably inadequate...Our memorial attempts to present a new idea of memory as distinct from nostalgia... We can only know the past today through a manifestation in the present."
>
> **Peter Eisenman,** Eisenman Architects

JUNE 1995 Artist Christine Jackob-Marks' design for a Memorial for the Murdered Jews of Europe is announced the winner. Her proposal features a 300-square-foot concrete slab engraved with names of the 4.2 million Jews identified by Israel's Yad Vashem Holocaust Memorial. It is later rejected by German Chancellor Helmut Kohl.

OCTOBER The Info-Box opens to the public and becomes one of Berlin's most popular attractions. With nearly two million visitors a year, the construction costs are covered by the $1 visitor's fee. The Info-Box

wins a number of architectural prizes including the 1996 Berlin Architekturpreis and the 1996 Deutsche Stahlbaupreis. **2 5 6**

1997

NOVEMBER 16 A second competition is announced for a Memorial for the Murdered Jews of Europe. The controversial project has caused fractious debate during the last ten years over the size of the site allocated to the memorial and the dominating presence it will have on the heart of Berlin.

1999

JUNE 26 Peter Eisenman and Richard Serra's proposal for the memorial is approved on the condition that the design is scaled back to 2,700 columns. Richard Serra later pulls out of the competition feeling the reduction in scale dilutes the artistic concept.

A multi-story building is also added to the design that will house a library and a research center. The addition is an attempt to conciliate critics who

find Eisenman's scheme too stylized and ahistorical. The building, also designed by Eisenman, and referred to as the "Ort" (German for "place") will provide information about the memorial as well as other sites pertaining to the Holocaust around Berlin. The building will be set below grade under the southeast corner of the memorial. **10 11 12**

2000-02

DECEMBER The Info-Box is torn down to make way for building work on the south side of Leipziger Platz.

FALL 2002 Construction begins on the Memorial for the Murdered Jews of Europe.

2004

JANUARY 27 Expected date of completion of the memorial, on the 59th anniversary of the liberation of Auschwitz.

Info-Box
ARCHITECTS: Schneider + Schumacher Architekten
BUILDING CONTRACT: Baustellenlogistik Potsdamer Platz
PLANNING FOR SUPPORTING STRUCTURE: Bollinger + Grohmann, Frankfurt/Main
EXPERT PLANNING: Burckardt, Emch + Berger GmbH, Berlin
BUILDING SUPERVISION: Emch + Berger GmbH, Berlin
GENERAL CONTRACTOR: Magnus Müller Pinneberg GmbH

Master plan for the reconstruction of Potsdamer Platz
CLIENT: DaimlerChrysler AG
ARCHITECTS: Renzo Piano Building Workshop in association with Christoph Kohlbecker
CONSULTANTS: Boll & Partners; Ove Arup & Partners, IBF Dr. Falkner GmbH; Weiske & Partners; IGH; Schmidt Reuter & Partner; Müller BBM; Hundt & Partner; IBB Burrer; ITF Intertraffic; Atelier Dreiseitl; Krüger & Möhrle; P.L. Copat; Drees & Sommer

Memorial for the Murdered Jews of Europe
CLIENT: Stiftung Denkmal für die ermoderdeten Juden Europas
ARCHITECT: Eisenman Architects
LEAD DESIGNER: Peter Eisenman
PROJECT ARCHITECT: Richard Rosson
PROJECT COORDINATOR: Sebastian Mittendorfer

Water system in Marlene Dietrich Platz
CLIENT: City of Berlin / Debis Immobilien
WATER DESIGN: Atelier Dreiseitl
ARCHITECTS: Renzo Piano Building Workshop, Christoph Kohlbecker Consultants
PROJECT MANAGEMENT: Atelier Dreiseitl and Peter Hausdorf

info-center, new york

The following quotes are taken from a forum held in June 2002 to ask "How can New York design and distribute information on the changing future of Lower Manhattan?" Till Schneider, Partner, Schneider+Schumacher Architekten, described his winning design of the Info-Box for Berlin with an introduction by architect Laurie Hawkinson. Respondents included landscape and urban designer Diana Balmori; Alexander Garvin, Vice President for Planning, Design and Development, Lower Manhattan Development Corporation; and architect Hugh Hardy.

Laurie Hawkinson: There are many reasons why people go to the World Trade Center site, and there are many publics involved, it's not just one public or one constituency. There is a tremendous need for information so people know what's happening in and around Ground Zero in the broadest sense. We should be asking what vehicles will ensure that this unfolding transformation of site, process and discourse is displayed to all constituencies affected and interested in future developments in Lower Manhattan.

Till Schneider: By telling you something about the Info-Box we designed for Potsdamer Platz, I wish to show how we succeeded in creating a forum for looking forward without neglecting past events. But what was it? Architecture? Merchandising? Public Relations? Advertising? A symbol of unification? A building site office? A work of art? What was required was a sign that building was in progress. People could enter a three-dimensional object; a box, two stories high. It was bright red like a stop sign, and had large openings that altered its sense of scale. The timeline for the box was as follows: two weeks for the competition, three months of decision-making, three months of planning, and three months of construction time. 16,000 people visited it a day, more than 20 times the number expected.

Hugh Hardy: In New York, the World Trade Center site itself becomes a place of information. How can you look at the big hole and not want to know things—and if you come here for the first time, one of the most amazing thing is—where were the two towers? There ought to be something that orients you to where you are and what's happening, and inevitably, any aspect of this will become part of memorialization.

Diana Balmori: I see the Info-Box as a way of digitally mapping a site. I think it's an enormously important event for New York to be able to digitally map this site by expanding the "now" of it and making us aware of what is happening all the time.

Alexander Garvin: Hugh Hardy described a place where we could participate in restoring what we have lost: a place where people could find out about the WTC site, express their opinions about it, and participate in it. There's one part that everyone forgets—that New Yorkers have a great love for construction. What we need is not just a place that allows us to find out what is going to happen there, but a place for all of us to participate in regaining what we have lost.

Member of the audience: (Marian Starr Imperatore) Given all the complexities of the site, maybe, while the Info-Box does not need to be built directly on the former WTC site, it could be built for downtown. We should celebrate all the others things about downtown, the history, art and culture, and the Info-Box could evolve over time to give more information about what would be built at the site.

Member of the audience: So what if the city finds a space in a park and decides they're going to build an Info-Box; a democratic place where people can affect what's going to be built there? If it is going to happen, someone has to step up to the plate and do it.

berlin, memorials, and the renewal of the city

JAMES E. YOUNG in conversation with RAYMOND W. GASTIL

James E. Young, professor of English and Judaic studies at the University of Massachusetts at Amherst, is the author of *At Memory's Edge: After-Images of the Holocaust in Contemporary Art and Architecture* (2000), and served on the committee and jury for the Memorial to the Murdered Jews of Europe now under construction in Berlin.

Raymond W. Gastil: From your perspective as a conceptualizer, juror, and consultant to the Memorial to the Murdered Jews of Europe now under construction in Berlin, can a memorial contribute to the renewal of a city?

James E. Young: In Berlin, it was never a matter of either renewal or memory of the past, but of making Berlin's past a part of, even a foundation for its renewal. Some might even say a reason for renewal. After WWII, the Soviets took this approach to an extreme in the eastern sector of Berlin, actually leaving the bullet-pocked façades and remnants of wartime destruction in evidence. In West Berlin, while they left hundreds of markers of former synagogues and sites of deportation around the city, they also scrubbed away most of the evidence of war.

In conceptualizing a new memorial, I had the notion that renewing the city and remembering what had been lost, in fact, might now become part of the very same idea. This resonated with the people in Berlin. One of the first things we did as a part of the memorial process there was to survey the entire context of the new Berlin. Whatever we did for a memorial would necessarily be related to other projects rising around the city at that time, including a direct conversation with the rising of the Reichstag, and even with the wrapping of the Reichstag by Christo in 1995. That temporary project was a testament to Germany's strength and resilience and to their great sense of self-deprecation, to allow their greatest political and cultural icon to be wrapped, purged, and then unveiled yet again.

RWG **In a temporary memorial, the lightness of Christo's approach seems possible, and even Nadim Karam's temporary project in Beirut has a kind of whimsy in its playful forms. Yet in a permanent memorial, you can't, and at the same time monuments of the gravest seriousness risk becoming kitsch, through a failed attempt at seriousness, taking away from the memory of a tragic event.**

JEY Yes, the kiss of death for a memorial is its own self-seriousness—witness anything from some of the Nazi architecture to Soviet architecture, the Soviet memorial architecture in particular. At the core of apparently "light" projects like Christo's, or a current generation of holocaust memorials, is a process-oriented approach that one way or another throws back into the faces of the people who come, their own role for remembering. To some extent, Eisenman took these things into account, not answering the question of Germany's dilemma—how does a nation commemorate those murdered in its name—but rather to articulate this dilemma in the design in a way that he hopes will be indeterminate. There are as many ways into this memorial as there are entries on the grid, and then there are also numberless ways through this memorial: everyone will create their own path in memory. That underdetermined design is that lighter touch.

In addition, there will be a place of information, which will be built underneath, and that was always a point of contention. The place of information is now a relatively small 13,000-16,000 square foot museum built underneath the site. Now the designers have allowed the steles from Eisenman's design to sink into the document house, like stalactites coming down, so the space of memory will intersect the space of history.

RWG **What do you expect a 25-year-old Berliner to feel at the memorial?**

JEY He or she will end up with a sense of national gravity. Something must have really mattered to the government to memorialize a crime committed way before the 25-year-old was born. There's this discussion of this "leader"-kultur—the guiding culture of the new Europe coming out of Germany, and if Germany is going to be the leading cultural edge of this new

Europe and you want to be a good German, and yet being a good German means remembering what it means to have been a bad German. There is a paradox in here that drives a younger generation crazy.

What will the next generation think of this? Will they be somewhat self-congratulatory the way that our generation can be about remembering slavery? Possibly. We think we can remember slavery with no cost. We didn't do it. We congratulate ourselves for recalling what was done at the hands of—well, not even my ancestors.

RWG **You found compelling reasons for a place of information in Berlin. Should there be the same in New York, at Ground Zero? To me, there are two risks, first, trivializing the incident through a sensationalist exhibit, and second, presenting a historical incident without the historical complexity that a museum requires, but may not be appropriate to a memorial.**

JEY I don't know if any national memorial and museum site is as democratic and well balanced as the version that we'd like to see. Where an event begins is altogether arbitrary, but the story has to begin somewhere. Yet while this makes doing a museum extremely difficult, I'd still like to see commemorative spaces anchored in the events they are purporting to commemorate.

RWG **Regarding how a memorial works with the renewal of a city, did anyone in Berlin denounce the Holocaust Memorial for lowering property values, or depriving the city of revenues—an active issue for Lower Manhattan?**

JEY No, but it was very much a part of an overall plan where they were going to balance commercial and public space. The history of German architecture, even dating back to Nazi and pre-Nazi designs, worked very hard to combine shop space with their great public axes. Speer designed this axis as a place for triumphal marches, but it had to be undergirded by what he called living buildings with shops and places for people to live on this great axis.

RWG **Berlin is trying to be a memorial city, commercial city, cultural city, and all at once, and this is in that context. New York has a similarly complex agenda, and here, too, has at least a five-acre site to begin with.**

JEY There has to be negotiation, and it's going to be a negotiation between different groups. Whatever gets built here is going to be regarded as having a commemorative function. Even commercial space, even the new Guggenheim, even the City Opera—it's going to be regarded as part of the memorial. If it were not for the terrorist act, these things would not exist down there.

The most responsible renewal always makes part of its narrative the reasons and conditions under which it came into being. So a museum or, another term, as in Berlin, place of information, will tell people why what is here is here, how it got here, and what events occasioned this. And even then it will have to mark a beginning point of that story, and finding that beginning point of the story is going to be a negotiation between the families, the developers, and the cultural historians.

kobe

1 Volunteers built the Paper Church in Kobe, Japan SHIGERU BAN ARCHITECTS

2 Aerial view of earthquake damage to the elevated highway (January 1995) THE KOBE NEWSPAPER

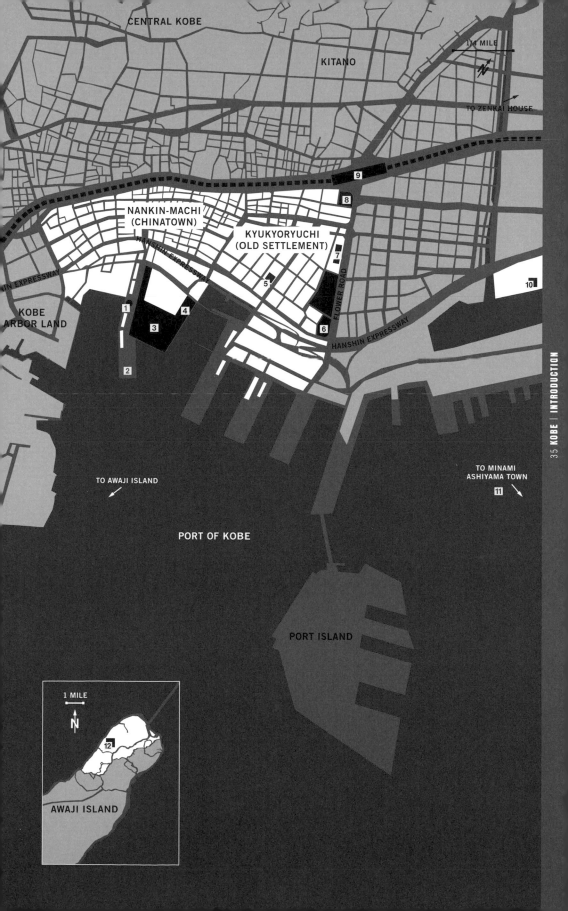

CENTRAL KOBE

KITANO

1/4 MILE

N

TO ZENKAI HOUSE

9

8

NANKIN-MACHI
(CHINATOWN)

KYUKYORYUCHI
(OLD SETTLEMENT)

HANSHIN EXPRESSWAY

HANSHIN EXPRESSWAY

7

FLOWER ROAD

5

10

KOBE
ARBOR LAND

1

4

3

6

2

HANSHIN EXPRESSWAY

TO MINAMI
ASHIYAMA TOWN

TO AWAJI ISLAND

11

PORT OF KOBE

PORT ISLAND

1 MILE

N

12

AWAJI ISLAND

kobe

In July of 1995, with a team of 160 local volunteers, Shigeru Ban began the construction of what has become known as the "Paper Church." This building, built from low-cost corrugated polycarbonate sheets on a steel scaffold, with an elliptical interior space made from 58 vertical paper tubes, has become the central emblem of Kobe's remarkable recovery from the earthquake, which struck the city with a magnitude of 7.2 on the Richter scale on January 17, 1995. The Great Hanshin-Awaji earthquake killed 6,000, injured 35,000 and left 300,000 homeless. Kobe, located in the second most populated area of central Japan near Osaka in Kansai, with a population of 1.5 million, is a major international port city. The port's operations were restored two years after the earthquake. In 1997 Kobe's Municipal Government announced Shingo Kusuda's design as the winner of an international competition for a memorial. Entitled "Cosmic Elements," the brick and glass sculpture, which houses a meditation room, was unveiled on the fifth anniversary of the earthquake. Also in memory of the event, the Kobe Port Terminal Corporation kept a section of a damaged pier as the Hokudan-Town Earthquake Memorial Park. More controversially, the Hyogo Prefectural Government decided to preserve a 492 foot portion of the exposed fault line of the earthquake in Hokudan Town on Awaji Island, just south of Kobe, by building a museum over it, and creating a research center for the study of earthquakes.

Since the emergency three-year housing plan was established in July 1995, approximately 200,000 new homes were built in the city and in December 1999, Kobe Municipal Government reported that all temporary housing residents in the city had moved into permanent public and private housing.

timeline> 1995

JANUARY 17, 5:46 a.m. The Great Hanshin-Awaji earthquake with a magnitude of 7.2 on the Richter scale hits south-central Japan in the region of Kobe and Osaka. Although it only lasts for a few seconds, 6,000 people die, more than half of whom are over 60 years old, and 35,000 people are injured. Approximately 300,000 people are left homeless. Evacuation shelters are opened immediately.

The region is Japan's second-most populated and industrialized area, after Tokyo, with a total population of about 10 million. The shock occurs at a shallow depth on a fault running from Awaji Island through the city of Kobe, which has a population of about 1.5 million. Strong tremors last for about 20 seconds and cause severe damage over a large area. Hyogo Prefecture, the state government for Kobe and Osaka, announces that 187,230 homes and buildings have been destroyed. Total estimated costs for repairs to buildings, the port, and infrastructure are reported at $100 billion. **2 3**

JANUARY 20 Kobe Municipal Government begins constructing emergency temporary housing made from

4

prefabricated units on parks, parking lots and school playgrounds.

JANUARY 23 Electricity is restored.

JANUARY 24 Kansai Architects Volunteer Group is established to diagnose the extent of the damage to housing. The group decides to propose a new housing plan that is in contrast to the government's plans to demolish all the damaged houses and replace them with high-rise apartment blocks.

JANUARY 25 Kobe Port Reconstruction Promotion Council is founded. The Port of Kobe, one of the largest container facilities in the world, saw most of its 239 berths, cranes and warehouses suffer severe damage. Kobe Municipal Government drafts the Kobe Port Harbor Plan. The goal is to rehabilitate its port facilities within two years.

FEBRUARY The Kobe Port Terminal Corporation (established in 1981) decides to keep a section of the damaged Meriken Park (completed in 1987) as a reminder of the earthquake. **4**

FEBRUARY 6 Victim Identification Certificates are issued.

FEBRUARY 15 Residents begin to move into pre-fabricated housing.

MARCH One million volunteers (more than 60% between the ages of 15 and 24) arrive from around the nation.

MARCH 31 Drinking water service is restored.

APRIL Japanese architect Shigeru Ban holds an exhibition in a department store to raise funds for a community building/church made from cardboard to replace the destroyed Takatori Church in Nagata-ku. The "Paper Church" is made from an outer layer of low-cost corrugated polycarbonate sheets mounted on steel scaffolding. Inside, an elliptical space made out of 58 vertical paper tubes is modeled after a baroque church by Bernini. **6**

APRIL 11 City gas is restored.

JULY Shigeru Ban and a team of 160 local volunteers, led by Koichi Wada, a, member of the parish, construct the Paper Church. **1**

Ban also develops the "Log House," made from cardboard tubes. The 170 square foot log houses rest on a foundation of donated beer crates filled with

Emergency housing made from paper tubes (July 1995)
HIROYUKI HIRAI

5

A steel brace is fixed to the front of the Zenkai House
ATELIER CINQUIÈME ARCHITECTS

7

The Paper Church (April 1995)
HIROYUKI HIRAI

6

Honda House
ARXKOBE

8

sandbags. Waterproof tapes made from strips of sponge with adhesive on both sides are placed between the tubes before they are squeezed together. The rectangular houses are estimated to cost $1,885 each. **5**

JULY 7 The Emergency Three-Year Plan for Housing Reconstruction is established. 12,500 new dwellings are to be constructed, with 8,500 dwellings designated as public housing.

Some of the city's architects research ways to save damaged houses. Katushiro Miyamoto of Atelier Cinquième Architects devises a system of steel girders and cross braces that he inserts into the existing wooden frame to reinforce the structure. Nobuaki Ishimaru of ARXKOBE designs the "Honda House" made from a steel frame with floor-to-ceiling windows and large open rooms that run the length of the building, divided by simple translucent doors. **7 8**

JULY 24 Given the overwhelming response from a large number of citizens who want to restore their homes rather than demolish them, the Kobe Housing Restoration Plan is established.

AUGUST 5 Kobe Municipal Government grants Shigeru Ban permission to build an additional 20 paper houses in Minami Komae Park.

AUGUST 20 Evacuation shelters close.

NOVEMBER A priority three-year Infrastructure Restoration Plan is approved.

1996

JANUARY Kobe Municipal Government forms a committee for a memorial dedicated to the lives lost during the earthquake. After four months of negotiation, the decision is made to build on a site just south of Kobe City Hall, in Higashi Park. The committee organizes a design competition and invites architects and artists Tadao Ando, Keiji Uematsu, Michio Fukuoka and Shingo Kusuda to submit proposals.

APRIL 4 The head office of the Post-Quake Citizen Support Services is established in Kobe.

JUNE 5 Citizens' Housing Restoration Council is established.

JULY The Comprehensive Plan for Relocation to Permanent Housing is approved. The plan aims to provide diverse, high-quality housing appropriate to an aging society.

JULY 11 The Hyogo Prefectural Government announces they will preserve a 492-foot portion of the fault of the earthquake in Hokudan Town on Awaji Island, south of Kobe. A museum is proposed, built over the section of the fault line. The surrounding area will be developed into the Nojima Earthquake Reconstruction Memorial Park. **9 10 11**

JULY 20 Rokko Island Ferry Terminal reopens.

AUGUST 24 Harbor Highway reopens.

OCTOBER 1 Reconstruction of Naka Pier is completed.

OCTOBER 18 The Port of Kobe trade zone (a 6.5 million square foot area on Port Island) is delineated in the Shanghai-Yangtze Trade Promotion Project.

DECEMBER Minami Ashiyahama Town (6 miles southeast of Kobe) Disaster Relief Public Housing Committee proposes a new housing development for victims of the earthquake.

> **"Human beings' coexistence with nature became the main concept of my design for this monument having witnessed people struggling during the earthquake but still able to retain hope for the future, regardless of their powerless existence in the devastated cities."**
>
> **Shingo Kusuda,** Sculptor

1997

JANUARY Sculptor Shingo Kusuda wins the Kobe Earthquake Memorial competition. His design, entitled "Cosmic Elements" consists of a 5,000-square-foot stone memorial with an underground meditation room. The stone walls of the meditation room are inscribed with the names of the people who died in the earthquake. **12 13**

MARCH 19 The Port of Kobe is restored.

APRIL 25 Payment begins of Socioeconomic Rehabilitation Aid as a Disaster Restoration Fund Project.

1998

JANUARY Monetary support for the three-year Industry Reconstruction Plan is expanded.

JANUARY 14 Kobe's Socioeconomic Rehabilitation Plan is devised.

FEBRUARY The Minami Ashiyahama Town housing development is approved and construction begins based on designs proposed by the City and State. The 814 units to be built will house 1,500 individuals, 60% of whom are senior citizens. Eleven architects and artists are invited to do public projects on the site. Public artist Ritsuko Taho is chosen to design a central park with land to grow crops.

MARCH 28 Minami Ashiyahama Town opens.

The City of Kobe announces that 81,500 new public housing units have been constructed in the city since the earthquake.

Hokudan-Town Earthquake Memorial Park and the Nojima Fault Museum are completed.

Massive earthquakes strike areas of Turkey and Taiwan. Japan donates 12,625 temporary housing units.

Construction of 134,000 more private housing units in Kobe begins.

JUNE 22 The Ministry of Transport approves the Kobe Municipal Government reclamation application for the airport-island. The Kobe Airport, which will have an 8,200 foot runway, will be built on a 170 mile-wide piece of reclaimed land about 2 miles south of Port Island at a cost of approximately $4.7 billion.

JULY Construction begins on "Cosmic Elements," the Kobe Earthquake Memorial.

JULY 30 Kobe Minatojima Tunnel (undersea tunnel linking Port Island and Shinko-Higashi Wharf) opens.

DECEMBER 20 Kobe Municipal Government reports that all temporary housing residents in the city have moved into permanent public and private housing.

Hyogo prefecture sends out a Request for Proposals for "The Great Hanshin-Awaji Earthquake Disaster Memorial, Disaster Reduction and Human Renovation Institute." The building will

"The museum was controversial. For some it was a painful reminder of the tragedy caused by the earthquake, but for others it was an opportunity to use the site as a research laboratory and learn more about the earthquake."

Tomoko Kawayoshi, Nojima Fault Museum

be a museum with artifacts from the earthquake, as well as a research center and a scientific library.

2000-01

JANUARY 17 "Cosmic Elements" is unveiled and Kobe Municipal Government establishes an annual candlelight vigil. Each year, 15,000 candles, mounted on bamboo, will be set to float on Kobe Bay. **14**

Hyogo Prefecture chooses Showa Sekkei Architects, Planners and Engineers' design proposal for The Great Hanshin-Awaji Earthquake Institute. Their design, a glass cube, will have a flexible interior.

SPRING-SUMMER 2001 Development of the 21st Century Kobe Restoration Commemorative Project begins.

2002

APRIL The Great Hanshin-Awaji Earthquake Disaster Memorial, Disaster Reduction and Human Renovation Institute opens. **15 16 17**

2005

Scheduled completion date of Kobe Airport.

Nojima Fault Museum
CLIENT: Hokudan Town, Awaji Island
DESIGNERS: Showa Sekkei Architects, Planners and Engineers

Kobe Earthquake Memorial
CLIENT: CITY of KOBE
DESIGNER: Shingo Kusuda

Minami Ashiyahama Disaster Recovery Public Housing Art Projects
DIRECTOR AND PUBLIC ART COORDINATOR: Toshiko Hashimoto
DIRECTOR OF PUBLIC ART: Hisako Hara
ART WORK AND ART WORKSHOP ADVISOR: Koichi Kawasaki
ART WORK SUPPORT TEAM: Tetsu Kubota and Kenichiro Yoshikawa

The Great Hanshin-Awaji Earthquake Disaster Memorial, Disaster Reduction and Human Renovation Institute
CLIENT: Hyogo Prefecture
DESIGNERS AND ENGINEERS: Showa Sekkei Architects, Planners and Engineers

re-mediating earth

YOSHIKO SATO

Yoshiko Sato is a Principal of Morris Sato Studio, New York, and a Visiting Assistant Professor in the Department of Architecture, Planning & Preservation at Columbia University. Morris Sato Studio is a prizewinner in the 2002 Home of the Year Awards Program of Architecture/Metropolitan Home. Sato received her BArch from The Cooper Union in 1989. Her 1996 thesis for her Master of Architecture from Harvard University's Graduate School of Design was entitled "New Urbanism and Housing in Kobe, Japan." In 2001 Sato revisited Kobe to research the city's redevelopment.

But the unforgiving truth is, they are running out of dirt to sift through at the World Trade Center site. The once monstrous task of debris removal and body recovery has come down to little more than a hill or two. It is the feeling of something at once depressing and darkly beautiful, and of a kind of twofold regret. (Eric Lipton and James Glanz, "In Last Piles of Rubble, Fresh Pangs of Loss," *The New York Times*, 17 March, 2002.)

The statement above describes Ground Zero recovery workers coming to terms with the completion of the rescue effort and in turn diminished hopes of finding the remaining one third of the victims of the WTC attack still uncovered. At Ground Zero, hope was buried in the earth. With dirt being the physical proof of one's memory, the workers simply wished they could make more of it. "But we can't make more dirt," said firefighter Keith J. Dillon. However, if the 98,000 truckloads of dirt were not removed from the Ground Zero site, the rebuilding of downtown New York could not start. The contradictory dilemma is that hope was embedded in the past. Hope and the future remained apart.

The meaning imbued in the earth at Ground Zero by the recovery workers and victims' families is difficult to comprehend and cannot be compared to any other kind of experience. Yet, when seen through the lens of the rebuilding of Kobe, seven years after the 1995 Great Hanshin-Awaji earthquake, new and positive trajectories emerge.

In the event and the aftermath of the Kobe earthquake, "earth" demonstrated its double nature— volatile and latent. The earthquake violently disrupted life and yet within the fault line itself, plants took root and became a metaphor for the healing process and eventual reconciliation of the past and the future. The destruction created by earthquakes and wars has historically played a major role in forming the urban landscapes of Japanese cities such as Tokyo and Kobe. The 1995 Great Hanshin-Awaji earthquake was the first to destroy a major post-war Japanese city. Coincidentally, the same year marked the fiftieth anniversary of the end of World War II. Kobe's pre-and postwar urban landscapes were completely erased by these two catastrophic events a half-century apart. Within a mere twenty seconds, the 1995 earthquake shattered the rapid economic achievements that had taken place in postwar Japan. One witnessed how short-lived the materialistic world is—and how illusory wealth can be when defined through one's physical possessions. The earthquake awakened some minds to elements often eclipsed by materialism that needed to be implemented in the process of renewing Kobe. Several of Kobe's rebuilding efforts addressed the importance of these long-forgotten elements, which are associated with a level of psychological space formed by either individual or collective consciousnesses.

After the earthquake, the memory of what had been destroyed inspired some local architects to conceptualize the reconstruction of the collapsed domestic environment. Katushiro Miyamoto of Atelier Cinquième Architects superimposed a new framework of steel bracing onto his 100 year-old family house to keep the broken wooden structure from collapsing—the spatial juxtaposition is intriguing and at the same time disturbing (p. 39). Miyamoto sealed the act of remembering (his own recollections of growing up in the house together with his new memories of the earthquake) in an improvised environment interfaced between old and new. In contrast, Nobuaki Ishimaru of ARXKOBE detached the memory of the earthquake from his house by treating the flattened ground as his departure and building a new structure made from decidedly non-domestic materials typically used to make industrial buildings (p. 39). The unconventional materials erased any physical reminder of the past, leaving one's personal memories intact. Inside, a loft-like void became a meditative space for the family to reflect on the past, as well as to project the future. Similarly, in the case of "Cosmic Elements," the earthquake memorial, a place to remember one's life was created, embracing the ground level of a public park (p. 41). The volume of moving water, suspended above the glass membrane that marks the horizon (ground), hovers above the meditation room below. "One of the most important aspects of the memorial is the meditation room," Shuji Fujita, a Kobe city official explains. "Sunlight enters through the water into the space where people can have an intimate moment, viewing or touching the names that are etched into the wall." A temporal phenomenon is infused by the multiple intersecting paths (both physical and psychological) that are drawn by both people and nature, continuously altered by the ever-changing forces of emotion, weather and time.

The memorial was inspired by having witnessed how one learns to coexist with nature and yet, is able to retain hope for the future regardless of the powerless existence of human beings in the devastated cities. (Sculptor Shingo Kusuda, the designer of "Cosmic Elements.")

As suggested in the title, "Cosmic Elements" positions itself away from the gravitational field and instead submerges a visitor's body into its underwater-like environment. One perceives nature as a light and ephemeral rather than a weighty physical reality. The dark side of physical reality, earth as an unstable mass that contributes to the brutality of nature, has been captured in the Nojima Fault Museum—a 450-foot long section of the fault line encased in a greenhouse-like structure (p. 40). The complicated scientific efforts and perhaps even the desire to save the fault line, which caused the earthquake, were not initially understood by people who had lived through the earthquake. Many feared that their painful memories would at once be permanently sealed within this frozen earth, yet remain active through the exposure of the fault line. It is impossible to detach the survivors' collective memories and at the same time keep the fault line for further studies in predicting earthquakes. Even though this fault (earth) reflects a moment of history, biologically scientists must simulate seasonal temperatures and solar exposure levels to keep plants and trees alive. Insects entering the museum and nesting inside of the preserved earth are not welcome. Scientists are continuously challenged to develop new chemicals to keep one type of life alive while terminating another.

"Kodoku-shi" (solitary death: individuals who are living alone and are discovered dead), suicide and alcoholism were frequently reported after earthquake victims were moved to live in temporary housing and

then moved again to disaster relief public housing. More than fifty per cent of the residents relocated were senior citizens who lost their houses as well as family members. They now live alone in single units in high-rise apartment blocks, next to strangers. Unfamiliar with living in high-rise buildings, they often complain of loneliness and isolation from social interaction. Used to one-or two-story houses they feel detached from the earth (ground). Reconstructing a psychological bridge between one's inner world and the outer material world, shattered in the disastrous events, requires more effort than simply reconstructing a physical place to live.

In the case of the Disaster Relief Public Housing project in Minami Ashiyahama Town (p. 34), built in 1998 on the newly developed landfill six miles southeast of Kobe city, earth not only had a symbolic role in forming public space, but also had a functional purpose, as a place to heal one's isolated soul. An unprecedented collaborative effort was made to save this housing project from becoming normative stacked up white concrete boxes surrounded by trees planted in a line. The Minami Ashiyahama Community Art Working Group brought developers, planners, contractors and volunteers together with architects and artists. Ten multi-scaled art commissions were proposed in order to foster an innovative public space for the housing community.

One of the public art projects is the garden terraces by Ritsuko Taho. Located in the middle of a housing complex, the land is not only used to grow flowers and crops but is also a meeting place for residents. Along with the construction of the terraces, countless efforts (a relatively invisible, slow and long-term process) to provide social events such as gardening workshops were critical to generating communication and deliberately implemented in the making of the housing community.

The 1995 earthquake left an enormous sense of loss. Yet, many discovered that the other side of earth—its capacity to generate and nurture life, could liberate one's mind from the tragic memory of the earthquake.

1 View of Exchange Square with water feature in center DIXI CARRILLO - EDAW, INC.

2 Urbis MANCHESTER CITY COUNCIL

manchester

MILLER STREET

SWAN STREET

1

CORPORATION STREET

2

3

SHUDEHILL

7

VICTORIA STREET

RIVER IRWELL

4

5

6

8

9

TIB STREET

HIGH STREET

11

10

12

13

MARKET STREET

15

14

LEVER STREET

PICCADILLY

ST. ANN STREET

CORPORATION STREET

MARKET STREET

PARKER STREET

16

CROSS STREET

PRINCESS STREET

17

PORTLAND STREET

PETER STREET

1/4 MILE

N

manchester

With damage assessed at close to one billion dollars, Manchester, a city of just under half a million residents situated 200 miles north of London, began its physical recovery from the IRA bombing of June 1996 with an invited international urban design competition for the selection of a master plan. Before the end of the year, the Manchester-based office of EDAW, a firm of landscape architects and urban planners was chosen to restore the damaged city center. Their vision specified that a new civic square would become the focus of the reconstruction effort to generate activity and figure as a central pedestrian thoroughfare connecting all areas of the city. In 1998, landscape architect Martha Schwartz's design for Exchange Square was chosen as the winner of the design competition. Within the multi-level gathering space, benches made from railway carts recall Manchester's history as the birthplace of the industrial revolution, while a water feature covered with stepping-stones recollects that the area was once a millrace. A further symbol of the city's recovery is Hodder Associates' new footbridge across Corporation Street, site of the bombing. Spanning 62 feet and made from a spiral of steel and glass, the covered walkway connects two shopping centers.

In addition to public space, the city seized the opportunity to renew the urban environment with new programs and fresh buildings, funded by private and public sector resources. Urbis was conceived of as part of the master plan and opened in June 2002. Within this shimmering glass object, designed by Ian Simpson Architects, inter-active displays enable visitors to explore what life is like in cities such as Singapore, Sao Paolo, Bombay and Los Angeles and engage in issues at the crux of contemporary urban life. With this project and a host of others, not all directly related to the post-bomb redesign but all planned since the bomb blast in 1996 (including the extended Manchester Art Gallery, the Daniel Libeskind-designed Imperial War Museum North, a Commonwealth Games stadium by Arup and the Lowry Centre, a theatre and art gallery complex by Michael Wilford & Partners) Manchester has reinvented itself as a cultural capital.

View of Corporation Street ooking south towards the site of the explosion and showing the damage to shops and the Corporation Street Footbridge
MANCHESTER CITY COUNCIL

3

49 MANCHESTER | TIMELINE

timeline> 1996

SATURDAY JUNE 15, 11:15 a.m. A 3,300 lb. bomb explodes in Manchester city center injuring 220 people in Britain's largest ever terrorist bombing. Police had begun to clear the area about forty minutes prior to the blast, after calls using a recognized IRA (Irish Republican Army) code word issued warnings to newspapers, radio stations and at least one area hospital. The blast, marked by a 40 foot by 15 foot deep crater, is centered at Corporation Street at the intersection of St. Mary's Gate and Market Street. A van carrying the bomb was parked directly outside the Marks & Spencer store at the Corporation Street entrance. The radius of damage extends over half a mile. Some 200,000 square feet of prime retail space and 300,000 square feet of office space is lost. Over 670 businesses are forced to close or relocate and homes in the Arndale Centre are declared inaccessible. Damage estimates are in excess of $980 million. 3

The rebuilding of Manchester is immediately recognized as a national priority and within weeks, the Government and Manchester City Council have

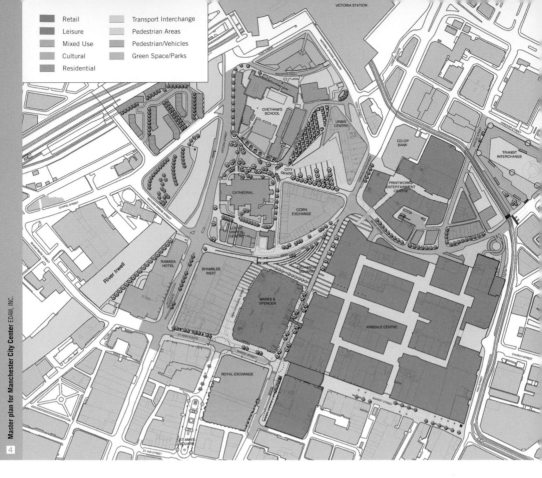

4

established a public and private sector task force Manchester Millennium Ltd. to develop and manage a recovery strategy.

JUNE 24 Manchester City Council stages a street party in Albert Square to celebrate the return to business.

JULY 3 The Home Secretary Michael Howard during his second visit to Manchester announces a $31.5 million aid package and an international urban design competition for a master plan for the city.

JULY 5 "Rebuilding Manchester: The Debate." A two and a half hour discussion about the needs of the city is held with 500 people at the University of Manchester Institute of Science and Technology.

JULY 29 Millennium Manchester Ltd. (MML) is formally established to oversee the relocation of businesses and the provision of financial assistance and direct the rebuilding framework, including the design competition to produce a master plan.

The Department of Transport, Local Government and the Regions, The European Regional Development Fund, Millennium Fund and private investors commit $653 million to the rebuilding of Manchester.

The Government and Manchester City Council propose six strategic objectives to direct the activities of the task force:

- Restoration and Enhancement of the Retail Core.
- Stimulation and Diversification of the City's Economic Base.
- Development of an Integrated Transport Strategy.
- Creation of a Quality City Core Fit for the 21st Century Creation of a Living City.
- The Creation of a Distinctive Millennium Quarter.

AUGUST 23 First round of design competition closes with 27 entries.

SEPTEMBER 4 Five firms are shortlisted. Each firm receives $30,000 and new guidelines for the second stage. Proposals are due on October 18.

SEPTEMBER 19 Council leaders announce a bid to secure $22.5 million from The National Lottery to help rebuild the city center.

SEPTEMBER 21 A 12-foot model of the city center master plan is displayed in the Shambles building for the public view. Their feedback on the redevelopment will be integrated into the design competition.

OCTOBER 18 The five short-listed competitors submit their second round of designs. Manchester Evening News joins with the development agency, Local Agenda 21, to announce a public forum for collecting views and ideas.

> "There was a great need for the city to reconstruct itself quickly. I wanted the Corporation Street Footbridge to be a symbol for Manchester's recovery after the bomb."
>
> Stephen Hodder, Principal, Hodder Associates

OCTOBER 25 The five shortlisted designs for a master plan go on display at Manchester Town Hall.

NOVEMBER 5 EDAW's master plan is announced the winner. Their team includes Jan Simpson, Alan Baxter (transport and engineering), Beroy (retail development), Hillier Parker DLE, and Johnson UDC. Supplementary Planning Guidance is adopted to underpin the master plan and to give a spatial definition and statutory basis to the vision. 4

EDAW's master plan in summary:

- An enlarged flagship Marks & Spencer store to be rebuilt on its old site in Exchange Square. A walkway through Marks & Spencer and the adjacent Arndale Centre with a footbridge over Corporation Street will link the two buildings with pubs and restaurants in Shambles Square.

- The Arndale Centre will be remodeled.

- Corporation Street will be reserved for pedestrians and buses only, and a special 'bus loop' will be created around the center.

- A Trocadero is planned for Maxwell House, with a cinema and games complex. EDAW will also construct a cultural center on the current N.C.P. car park with a library and theater.

- In addition to repairing and remodeling existing buildings such as the Corn Exchange, new buildings, such as URBIS, a new museum for the modern city, will be built.

- During extensive public consultation sessions the key priority that arose was the creation of new safe

public spaces. These include Exchange Square, a new civic plaza that will turn a busy trafficked intersection into a contemporary square in the center of the city.

Out of the 670 businesses originally displaced by the bomb less than 70 still need to be relocated to temporary sites.

85% of the city center is open and trading.

1997

SPRING The Old Wellington Inn is relocated brick by brick to a new site approximately 200 yards from its former home to make way for the construction of Exchange Square and the new Marks & Spencer building. **7 8**

SEPTEMBER MML announces an invited design competition for Exchange Square, a new civic plaza.

DECEMBER Hodder Associates wins design competition for a new footbridge across Corporation Street connecting the extended Arndale Centre and the new

> **"Inside Urbis, visitors will be able to explore how cities have changed the way people live, work and play together, and find out about life in cities as varied as Singapore, Sao Paolo, Bombay and Los Angeles."**
>
> Warren Smith, Chairman of Manchester's Millennium Quarter Trust

Marks & Spencer stores at the heart of the city center. The bridge spans 62 feet and is an hourglass shaped spiral of steel and glass with an oak bridge. **5 6**

1998

JANUARY Landscape architect Martha Schwartz is chosen as the designer of Exchange Square. Her design will link the new retail and entertainment quarter with the old medieval part of the city and calls for a multi-level plaza. **1 9**

MARCH Ian Simpson Architects is announced the winner of an international competition sponsored by Manchester City Council to design Urbis, a new "museum for the modern city." A group of representatives from the academic, private and public sectors of the city, led by Dr. Justin O'Connor, Director of the Manchester Institute of Popular Culture, begin research and development into the concept for the museum, which will cost $63 million and will be housed in a 115 foot-high glass-skinned building overlooking Exchange Square. **2 10 11 12**

Urbis with passing tram JAN CHLEBIK

Funicular in Urbis MANCHESTER CITY COUNCIL

Exhibition displays in Urbis NICK WOODS/ GRAHAM CARLOW

SPRING Construction begins on the Printworks entertainment complex.

SUMMER Construction begins on the 1.3 million square foot remodel of the Arndale Centre.

AUGUST Millennium Quarter, the area being developed around Urbis and the Cathedral secures $30 million from The National Lottery.

NOVEMBER Refurbishment of the Corn Exchange begins.

DECEMBER Manchester Millennium Ltd. announces international competition for the redesign of Piccadilly Gardens.

1999

MARCH International design consultants DEGW are appointed as exhibition coordinator and master planner for Urbis. Exhibition designers At Large, Land Design Studio and Event Communications, are hired to undertake extensive research and design development.

May EDAW are selected to develop the master plan for the redesign of Piccadilly Gardens. The design team is led by Arup, Chapman Robinson Architects, lighting designer Peter Fink and cost consultants Davis Langdon Everest. The scheme will include a central elliptical fountain spanned by a catwalk bridge and new horticultural gardens planted next to an existing statue of Queen Victoria. A curved pavilion designed by Tadao Ando and made from concrete, will shelter the park from the Parker Street bus station and the tramlines to the south, and will house a café and an information center.

SPRING Renovation of the relocated Old Wellington Inn is complete.
Construction begins on the transport Interchange, a new Metrolink/Bus passenger transport interchange at Shudehill.

NOVEMBER Exchange Square and New Cathedral Street are completed.

NOVEMBER 22 A red Victorian post box, the only piece of Corporation Street to have withstood the explosion, is ceremonially re-installed by Manchester's Lord Mayor.

New flagship Marks & Spencer designed by Building Design Partnership opens.

NOVEMBER 25 The Corporation Street Footbridge linking Marks & Spencer and the Arndale Centre opens.

DECEMBER Printworks Leisure Scheme is completed.

Corn Exchange Retail Scheme is completed.

2000-02

February Construction begins on Urbis.

MARCH 2001 Construction begins on Piccadilly Gardens and Pavilion.

MAY 2002 Piccadilly Gardens opens.

JUNE 27 Urbis opens.

2004

Expected completion date of the transport interchange.

Master Plan
MASTER PLANNING CONSULTANTS AND DESIGN CO-ORDINATION: EDAW, Inc.
TRANSPORTATION CONSULTANTS: Oscar Faber
COST CONSULTANTS: Davis Langdon Everest
PROGRAMME MANAGERS: MACE
PUBLIC REALM WORKS: EDAW, Inc.
EXCHANGE SQUARE: Martha Schwartz, Inc.
CITY PARK: EDAW, Inc. and Building Design Partnership
URBIS: Ian Simpson Architects

URBIS
CLIENT: Manchester City Council Special Projects Team
ARCHITECT: Ian Simpson Architects
PROJECT MANAGERS: Manchester City Council Special Projects Team
PROJECT ADMINISTRATORS: MPM Capita Ltd.
BUILDING CONTRACTOR: Laing NW
STRUCTURAL ENGINEERS: Martin Stockley Associates, Halcrow Waterman
M & E ENGINEERS: Farley McGrath Consulting Engineers
QUANTITY SURVEYORS: Davis, Langdon & Everest
CONCEPT DEVELOPMENT: Dr. Justin O'Connor, Director of the Manchester Institute of Popular Culture, and DEGW
EXHIBITION DESIGNERS: At Large, Land Design Studio, Event Communications

Corporation Street Footbridge
ARCHITECTS: Hodder Associates
STRUCTURAL ENGINEERS: Arup
CONSTRUCTION MANAGER: Bovis Construction Ltd.

Exchange Square
LANDSCAPE ARCHITECTS: Martha Schwartz, Inc.
LOCAL TECHNICAL TEAM: Urban Solutions Manchester

urbis

DR. JUSTIN O'CONNOR in conversation with Zoë Ryan

Dr. Justin O'Connor is Director of the Manchester Institute of Popular Culture at Manchester Metropolitan University and was lead academic advisor for Urbis, Manchester.

Zoë Ryan: Urbis, "the museum of the modern city," which opened in June 2002 was conceived of as part of Manchester's master plan that was developed after an IRA bomb destroyed the city center in 1996? How did your involvement in the project come about?

Dr. Justin O'Connor: The master plan merely indicated a cultural and/or visitor based attraction. A number of options were explored—a theater, a contemporary art gallery, a music venue—but all were deemed inappropriate for a number of reasons (I was not involved at this point). The wider context is that since the late 1980s the city council had already moved from a position of confrontation with the central (conservative) government, based on a left leaning labor politics, to one of cooperation and collaboration. This led to the emergence of many public-private partnerships and a general sense of a new permeability in decision-making. One interesting aspect of this is that culture was embraced as central to Manchester's regeneration vision, which meant that this permeability was not restricted to large-scale developers but included small-scale developers and cultural activists with a commitment to the future of the city. Many of these had been involved in Manchester's music, design and restaurant/bar/club scene in the late 1980s.

One of these people, Tony Wilson (now the central figure in Michael Winterbottom's film "24 Hour Party People") came forward with an idea for the post-bomb space called "POP," a museum of popular culture. A meeting to discuss the proposal was called and I was invited because of my involvement with the Institute for Popular Culture. At that meeting I suggested that "popular culture" might be a bad idea for a museum—the definition was too contentious and the contents lacked focus—but what people seemed to want to celebrate was contemporary urban culture; Manchester's past as an urban rather than simply "industrial" city and its revival as a place of urbanity and culture. I wrote a five-page treatment of this theme and faxed it the next morning. The vision statement became the basis of a lottery bid. This was then fleshed out into an architectural competition, won by Ian Simpson Architects.

I was not involved in the latter stages of the bid or the competition. I was brought back into the process as the development of content moved center stage after the building work commenced. I developed the vision statement, worked with DEGW who helped develop the exhibition design brief, and as part of a small client team group, I oversaw the development of the exhibition design up to installation.

ZR Is Urbis financed by both private and public funds?

JO The building, which had a budget of approximately $45 million, was funded by lottery monies (The Millennium Commission) and the European Regional Development Fund. Its operating finance comes from tickets, sponsorship, commercial activities and approximately $1.5 million per year from Manchester City Council. The public sector in the form of the city steered the whole museum through. It was generally welcomed as useful in terms of helping to regenerate the city center.

ZR What is the focus of Urbis?

JO So many museums related to the city focus on either socio-economic history—taking this in terms of history of class, gender and ethnic groupings and ways of life—or the built environment (morphology and architecture). We did not want to exclude these issues but were interested in looking at the experiential aspect of urban living—how cities change peoples' structure of experience. And we wanted to say something about how Manchester played a key role in this story.

ZR Urbis was designed by the Manchester-based office of Ian Simpson Architects who won the international design competition in 1998. Their design is one of the few island-buildings in Manchester. The dramatic form of the monolith, made from a glass skin of 2,200 panels, sweeps steeply from the height of a single story on the rear side of the building to 115 feet at the front. As well as a gift shop, café, education and corporate entertainment spaces, and a restaurant and bar on the fifth and sixth floors with views over the city, one of the main attractions of the building is the indoor funicular which takes visitors to the fourth floor—with unobstructed views of the city on the way up—and the start of the museum. From there visitors make their way down the building through a series of linked exhibitions. The following statement by Dr. Justin O'Connor explains the program of the museum.

JO Urbis is organized around four main story lines that give a broad narrative structure to the exhibitions as a whole.

- The rapid and often shocking growth of the modern city as industry moved from the countryside to the town.

- How the growth of the city transformed our culture, our experience, bringing a new way of life.

- How the growth of the modern city presented radical challenges to the existing order of cities—new fears and anxieties brought forth new discourses and techniques concerned ordering and controlling the big city populations and the spaces they inhabited.

- How the modern city demanded new ways of understanding the city, new ways of representing often confusing and scary realities. But it also gave an imaginative challenge—stimulating artists and writers and musicians to deal with this new subject matter, as well as forming the basis for the explosion of mass popular culture.

Arrive (Level 4) looks at the experience of entering the city—from the point of view of migrants, but also the more everyday arrival of commuters, tourists, those in search of fun, etc. In *Arrive* we see the city made "readable" by abstract signs and images. But as we come to know the city we create our own "mental maps," we personalize the city—different places have different associations—we "customize" it.

Change (Level 3) is about making sense of the city, making it your own. This is primarily about forming social ties—different ethnic/national groups form an important part of this story. These stories are told through the experiences of particular groups and individuals and those of others across the globe and in the past. The forming of social ties is not just about migrant groups—the modern city has seen the proliferation of many types of social connections—religious and political associations, youth cultures, sporting affiliations, gay and lesbian cultures, and the kaleidoscopic range of interests and passing associations called "lifestyle cultures."

Order (Level 2) continues to focus on personal experience, but does so in the context of the city as a complex system. The growth of the modern city presented radical challenges to the existing order of cities—new fears and anxieties brought forth new discourses and techniques concerned to order and control the big city populations and the spaces they inhabited. These challenges were also part of the wider transformation of experience—new forms of behavior, new public spaces, new living places, and new working and leisure patterns. *Order* has five main sections. "The Square" looks at public spaces and the control of the city; "Urbis Court" is about private spaces, but ones we partly share with the strangers we live amongst; "Mean Streets" is about urban fears, real and mythical; "Out of Control" about those marginal spaces of the city and those who inhabit them; "Control Zone" looks at techniques of surveillance and tracking in the city.

Explore (Level 1) is the largest floor and has two sections, "Imagining the City" and "Urbisville". Imagining the City is a large interactive database of novels, music, computer animation, film stills, architectural design, etc. involving four large surfaces across which thumbnail images flow. The visitor selects one of these by touching it and it appears in large scale on the desk, and is also projected onto a large cityscape created by an Austrian computer artist from Arts Electronica in Linz. The visitor gets an image and/or sound excerpt, plus some information text. The visitor contributes to the evolving cityscape of the different images selected, which form a "city of imagination" to floats above "Urbisville" in the adjoining space.

"Urbisville" is a city grid made up of a cross referencing of 6 cities (Manchester, Paris, Tokyo, Singapore, Los Angeles and Sao Paolo) and five themes (Sensing/Seeing; Moving; Working; Playing; Renewing). Where each intersects a different aspect of both city and theme is explored. "Manchester Playing" looks at the rise of organized sport in the industrial city. "LA Playing" looks at the erosion of the line between leisure and work. "Sao Paolo Moving" takes a helicopter ride over the city, looking at gated communities and favelas. "Singapore Moving" looks at import/export as the basis of its economy, as well as its strict control over the moving of material such as drugs, people and information. "Manchester Seeing" looks at the role of pop music in re-imagining the city. "Tokyo Seeing" looks at the complex street patterns

and signage showing its relationship to an older non-western system of urban organization.

ZR Does the museum have a space for temporary, rotating installations aside from the permanent exhibitions?

JO Yes it does. The plans so far are to build in exhibitions, which explore in more detail the issues raised in the main exhibitions. They will also be linked to the educational program, which aims to use Urbis as a central focus for debate and exchange on the subject of the city.

ZR How did you choose the cities explored in Urbis? Did you use a particular selection process?

JO We took these cities as exemplars of a particular history and/or position in a global network of cities. Manchester is the post-industrial city, looking to reinvent itself. Paris is the classic capital city, accumulating culture and highly branded cultural consumption capital. Los Angeles is the postmodern city, the center of image production, representing a challenge to eurocentric notions of what a city should be. Tokyo is an example of the Eastern city, which developed along lines whose internal logic derived from a non-Western dynamic. It is also a global financial capital, one central to the contemporary global nexus of flows. Singapore is a highly controlled city—using ultra modern planning and production techniques but in a context far removed from our notions of "the polis." Sao Paolo is on the fault line between developed and underdeveloped—in fact reproducing these lines within its own spaces. It is also a Latin city, which allowed us to look at this distinct urbanism associated with Latino cultures. Bombay and St. Petersburg play relatively minor roles in the exhibit. Bombay as an Indian city of sprawl and chaos; St. Petersburg as a post-communist city.

ZR The museum is defined as a place where people can "experience an ever-changing urban world by interacting with different cities from around the globe." You coordinated the exhibitions with John Williams, the museum consultant, can you explain the design of the exhibitions and what visitors will experience and learn from them?

JO The exhibition is based around audio-visual presentations—from simple text and image, through different forms of interactive projects, right through to computer based interactive elements. There is no "collection" in the form of historical objects. The museum in this sense is about the organization of ideas. We are also clear that the object—the city—is a vast, multi-faceted and complicated object that presents enormous problems for interpretation. Urbis does not attempt to represent the city and its spaces in a direct way—nor reduce it to a schematic overview or diagrammatic representation. It tries to give a glimpse into the experiential dimensions of urban living, although we are also clear that group and individual experiences are structured by larger forces. Urbis makes the visitor think about the city, to become aware of it around them, to leave the museum and see the real city anew.

ZR How important are architectural landmarks, such as Urbis, to a city's identity?

JO Architectural landmarks are very important, but often unpredictable. The Eiffel Tower only became so grudgingly. Some Stalinist monuments will disappear without a tear being shed. Manchester lacks such iconic buildings and Urbis is set to become one for the city.

9:01

oklahoma city

1 View of the Eastern Gate of the Oklahoma City National Memorial ANTHONY L. LINDSEY

2 Aerial photo of Oklahoma City prior to the 1995 bombing ACE AERIAL PHOTOGRAPHY, INC.

oklahoma city

On Wednesday April 19, 1995 at 9:02 a.m., a 4,800lb ammonium nitrate and fuel oil bomb exploded in a parked truck outside the
Alfred P. Murrah Federal Building in downtown Oklahoma City killing
168 people and wounding 500 others. Over 300 buildings were damaged. During a two year process that was unprecedented in America,
Oklahoma City citizens dedicated themselves to the memorialization
of the victims and the renewal of the city through urban planning and
new building, including a redesigned Federal Building currently being
constructed on an adjacent site to its original, now the location of
the Oklahoma City National Memorial, and due to be completed in
fall 2003. Three months after the rescue operations had ceased on
the bombed site, a 350-member task force was organized to initiate
an open process to memorialize those lost. An international design
competition organized by the advisory committee of the task force
drew a total of 624 designs. Of these, 400 were publicly displayed to
the residents of Oklahoma City. On June 24th 1997, the winning entry
was chosen by a jury of family members, survivors, community leaders
and design professionals. Butzer Design Partnership's project is
heavily symbolic, charting the minutes flanking the bomb's explosion.
168 empty chairs for each of the victims of the blast fill one field
and a surviving elm tree represents the resilience of the city and its
inhabitants. Hans E. Butzer explains: "We had to think about what this
event meant, and how we wanted to embody that meaning in design.
We needed to isolate what happened, isolate the meaning of the event—
pain and healing were at the heart of the design."

Aerial photo of Oklahoma City after the 1995 bombing, with Alfred P. Murrah Federal Building at center ACE AERIAL PHOTOGRAPHY, INC.

3

61 OKLAHOMA CITY | TIMELINE

timeline> 1995

WEDNESDAY APRIL 19, 9:02 a.m. A 4,800lb ammonium nitrate and fuel oil bomb explodes in a parked truck outside of the Alfred P. Murrah Federal Building in downtown Oklahoma City killing 168 people and wounding 500 others. When the catastrophe occurs, about 600 federal and contract workers and about 250 visitors are in the building. The force of the blast damages 324 surrounding buildings and blows out windows and doors in a 50-block area, though the most intense impact is within a three to four block radius. Overall, approximately 200 blocks are affected in the downtown area. News reports indicate the explosion is felt 55 miles from the site and registers 6.0 on the Richter scale. Built in 1977, the Murrah Federal Building housed numerous federal agencies. People immediately start gathering blocks away to make offerings of poems, cards, and flowers. **2 3 4**

APRIL 23 Tens of thousands attend prayer services at the State Fair Arena, the Made in Oklahoma Building, and the All Sports Stadium on a day of national mourning. The rescue effort continues.

MURRAH DISTRICT REVITALIZATION PROGRAM
Applications for Damage Repairs

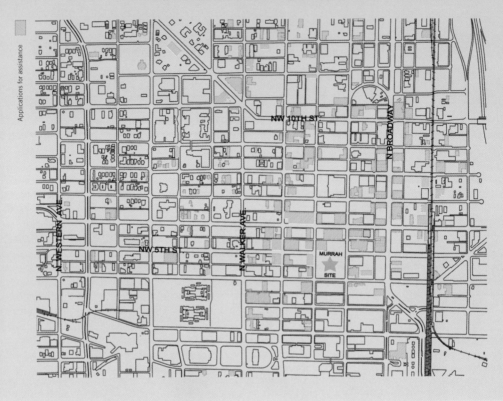

MAY 4 Rescue operations cease at 11:30 p.m.

Mayor Ron Norick invites Robert Johnson, a well-known local attorney, to develop an organizational plan for a diverse 350-member memorial task force, including bombing survivors, rescuers, and relatives of the dead, and civic leaders.

Victims' family members and mourners create a makeshift memorial from a chain-link fence erected to keep people off the site.

MAY 23, 7:00 a.m. The ruins of the Murrah Federal Building are imploded.

The objectives of the memorial task force are to create and administer a planning process resulting in a design recommendation to Mayor Ron Norick and the City Council, and to provide funding for completion and possibly ongoing administration and maintenance of the memorial.

Task force organizational structure:

- An Advisory Committee made up of a broad-based coalition representative of citizens from all con-stituencies affected by the bombing.

- Ten Operating Subcommittees: Administration, Archives, Budget, Design Solicitation, Government Liaison, Memorial Ideas Input, Public and Private Grants, Public Relations, Public Fund Raising, and Victims' Families/Survivors Liaison.

- A Coordinating Committee.

JUNE 16 National Endowment for the Arts offers to sponsor a national design workshop to generate ideas for redeveloping the bomb-affected area. Oklahoma City citizens are asked to submit ideas for rebuilding a 190-acre area surrounding the bomb site.

JULY 6 The three host agencies for the design work-shop: the City Planning Department, Urban Renewal Authority/Second Century Development and the Arts Council of Oklahoma City hold a planning meeting attended by local stakeholders, property and business owners, design professionals and financiers. Over the next three weeks they develop their recommendations to present on July 24-25.

JULY 24-25 The national panel convenes and prepares a final report.

The final report is presented to the media and the public. Recommendations include that government

Aerial photo of Oklahoma City National Memorial (1999) ACE AERIAL PHOTOGRAPHY, INC.

5

63 OKLAHOMA CITY | TIMELINE

functions be returned to the area, a national memorial on the site be developed, open spaces be enhanced, building codes be modified and residential development be encouraged in the area.

JULY 26 Orientation for the memorial task force is held at St. Luke's Methodist Church.

U.S. Congress allocates $39 million for recovery and rebuilding efforts. All funds are disbursed through the Department of Housing and Urban Development's (HUD) Block Grant Program.

SUMMER 1995-SPRING 1996 Members of the memorial task force conduct an intensive and inclusive listening process to gather ideas from families, survivors and the general public throughout the world about what visitors to the memorial should feel and experience.

1996

MARCH 26 The advisory committee of the memorial task force unanimously approves the mission statement drafted to guide the design and development of the memorial.

JULY The memorial task force holds a public meeting to explain the memorial design competition process.

FALL 1996 The original memorial task force becomes the Oklahoma City Memorial Foundation. From the onset, the Foundation is determined to raise the majority of the needed $30 million from private resources.

NOVEMBER 15 The Memorial Foundation announces an open international design competition for the Oklahoma City Memorial. Requests for entry materials are received from all 50 states and around the world.

NOVEMBER 16 "We Will be Back: Oklahoma City Rebuilds" opens at The National Building Museum in Washington, DC, and runs through March 17, 1997.

1997

MARCH 11 Deadline for memorial designs. 624 designs are submitted from 24 countries, including 144 from Oklahoma City. Over 400 design boards qualify for consideration, and go on public display in the Oklahoma City Hardware Building.

APRIL 19 The Memorial Foundation's nine-member evaluation panel chooses five finalists: James Rossant and Richard Scherr of New York City; Susan Herrington and Mark Stankard of Iowa State University; J. Kyle Casper and Brian Bransetter of Dallas, Texas; Hanno Weber, Kathleen Hess, and Michael Maher of Chicago, Illinois; and Hans and Torrey Butzer and Sven Berg of Berlin, Germany.

JUNE 24 A jury made up of eight family members and survivors, three community leaders, and four design professionals choose the Butzer/Berg design as the winner.

The final design for the outdoor portion of the memorial is comprised of seven primary components. Twin "Gates of Time" at each end of the site symbolize 9:01 and 9:03, the minutes flanking the bomb's explosion. **1 5**
A sweeping reflecting pool occupies what was formerly 5th Street and connects the gates. Representing the

> "The Oklahoma City memorial process represented something quite significant in the history of public memorialization. Many memorials, of course, exist to offer comfort, assuage grief, and inspire future generations to emulate the virtues ostensibly enshrined in memorials. It would be hard to find a memorial process, however, that included over three hundred people, many of whom had just suffered traumatic loss. ...[it] served as an ingeniously designed model of community consensus building."
>
> Edward T. Linenthal Published in *The Unfinished Bombing: Oklahoma City in American Memory* (Edward T. Linenthal, Oxford University Press, 2001).

168 victims, a grid of bronze and illuminated glass chairs, each inscribed with a name, occupies a field that had once been the Murrah Federal Building. On the surviving east wall of the building, carved in granite salvaged from the rubble, are the names of those who survived. A promontory surrounds the Survivor Tree, an American elm that survived the bomb blast. A Children's Area remembers the many messages of support from young people. Between the Survivor Tree and the Children's area, an orchard honors the rescuers and volunteers. **8**

FALL 1997 The Oklahoma City National Memorial Act moves through Congress to establish the Oklahoma City National Memorial and the creation of the Oklahoma City National Memorial Trust.

Final cost estimates place the repair of buildings and infrastructure at more than $150 million.

A temporary memorial, which was later incorporated into the permanent Oklahoma City National Memorial JOSHUA GELFMAN

7

The Survivor Tree at Oklahoma City National Memorial ANTHONY L. LINDSEY

8

1998

MARCH 13 Dedication of the new Central Post Office to replace the one lost in the bombing.

OCTOBER 25 Several hundred people attend the groundbreaking ceremony for the memorial site.

OCTOBER 26 Private ceremony for families, survivors, and rescue workers to relocate several large sections of the chain-link fence memorial to its new location near the western gate, the "healing" side of the Memorial. **7**

1999

JANUARY 28 The design for the Oklahoma City National Memorial Center, developed by community volunteers and the staff of the Memorial Center, is announced. Housed in the Journal Record Building, which forms the north wall of the memorial, the Oklahoma City National Memorial Center has three components: the outdoor memorial, a museum, and an institute for the prevention of terrorism.

2000

APRIL 19 President Clinton dedicates Oklahoma City National Memorial. 500,000 people visit the memorial in the first year. **6**

2001

FEBRUARY 16-18 A preopening of the Memorial Center is held for directors, family members, survivors, rescue workers and the press.

FEBRUARY 19 President Bush opens Memorial Center. Over 300,000 people visit in the first year.

MAY 18 A groundbreaking ceremony is held for the new U.S. Federal Campus located one block northwest of the former site in north downtown, bound by 6th and 8th Streets and Harvey and Hudson Avenues. The 180,000-square-foot office building, part of a two-block $40-million U.S. Federal Campus, is designed by Ross Barney + Jankowski Architects of Chicago.

In their design, the northern lobby entrance provides a gateway to the city's downtown, and the southern gives access to government buildings on the other side.

2003

SEPTEMBER Scheduled completion date of the new U.S. Federal Campus.

Oklahoma City National Memorial
CLIENT: Oklahoma City Memorial Foundation
DESIGNERS: Butzer Design Partnership, Hans Butzer, Torrey Butzer, and Sven Berg

Oklahoma City National Memorial Center
CLIENT: Oklahoma City National Memorial Trust
DESIGNERS: Oklahoma City National Memorial Center Staff,
Oklahoma City Community, Exhibit Concepts, Inc.
VIDEO/INTERACTIVE COMPONENTS: Hillman & Carr, Inc.

Federal Campus
CLIENT: U.S. General Services Administration
DESIGNERS: Ross Barney + Jankowski, Inc., Atkins Benham
CONSTRUCTION MANAGER: Heery International
CONSTRUCTION: Flintco, Inc.

voices from oklahoma city

As with the timelines featured in the exhibit and catalogue, the following articles offer a specific viewpoint at a specific moment in time, illuminating the process of urban change. The first article describes how the city, while still in shock, was nonetheless moving forward with plans for the memorial and renewing downtown Oklahoma City. The second article, written three years after the first, and a year after National Memorial opened, portrays a city where the focus has changed from abstract aspirations for a future memorial to the practical realities of a national memorial and evolving downtown district that attracts hundreds of thousands of visitors each year.

"Past Shadowing Efforts to Rebuild Oklahoma City Three Years Later, Some Eager to put Bombing Behind Them," by Arnold Hamilton, *The Dallas Morning News*, April 19, 1998

OKLAHOMA CITY - At civic club luncheons where he speaks, Oklahoma City bombing survivor Paul Heath asks a simple, yet provocative question: "How many of you wish that survivors and family members and people like me and the media would stop talking about this?"

"There'll be about 20 percent just shoot up their hands, and I just say to them, I understand that feeling. But let me tell you our side of it," Dr. Heath says. "I wish it could fade for the rest of us, but it won't. And it can't."

Three years after a truck bomb pulverized the Alfred P. Murrah Federal Building and ravaged 18 square blocks of downtown, Oklahoma City still grapples with the disaster—unable and unwilling to forget yet craving to move on and escape the yoke of a City of Grief. Publicly and privately, potent forces are at work here, alternately guiding and prodding Oklahoma City into a future in which the city might be known more for a revitalized downtown and quality of life than for the tragedy. "We can't dwell on the past - we do have to continue on," said Jim Brewer, a leading developer of the city's warehouse-turned-entertainment district known as Bricktown. "The silver lining in all this is that we're not a cowboy or Indian reservation state anymore. We're a living, breathing, sophisticated metropolitan city that's on the move." Decaying buildings and those damaged in the bombing are slowly being replaced by a new ballpark and sports arena, high-rise hotels, and a three-

square-block federal complex. But at the same time, vivid reminders of America's worst act of domestic terrorism endure.

Sunday's anniversary of the April 19, 1995, workday attack that killed 168 stokes painful memories for many. State murder trials for Timothy McVeigh and Terry Nichols are being discussed, even though the two were convicted by federal juries. And a county grand jury continues to investigate the case. But there are unmistakable signs that many want this city to focus more on the future and capitalize on the good will generated by Oklahoma City's response to the tragedy. As last week's opening of the $32 million Southwestern Bell Bricktown Ballpark neared, news releases were sent out nationally depicting the park's debut as a "milestone" in the city's recovery. "For the people of Oklahoma City, the symbolism as well as the reality of being 'back in the game' with this beautiful new baseball stadium will be lost on no one," one promotional release noted. Even as they encourage the momentum to move on, city leaders and residents choose their words carefully. Former Mayor Ron Norick, for one, addresses questions about the city's mood with the preface: "Not walking in somebody else's moccasins that had the loss of a family member or a really dear friend, it's hard to say, but I think generally…" Mr. Norick, whose 11 years as mayor ended last week, said he now sees a "much more heightened awareness of Oklahoma City than there was three years ago. Not to use the bombing—we don't want to use that—but…we need to tell people in the country more about who we are and what we're doing and how we're improving our quality of life and all those sorts of things. I think we're doing that."

Before the bombing, according to the former mayor, and Governor Frank Keating, national surveys showed the city and state had no enduring image in the American consciousness. Afterward, they said, Oklahoma City was renowned for its professionalism, sense of community, goodness and sacrifice. "That gave the world a view of Oklahoma that had never been," Mr. Keating said in an interview. "But it gave Oklahomans a view of themselves that never existed. We turned on the television set, and all of the sudden we saw ourselves as really very gifted, professional, competent. These were not the Joad family. If we can use that as a trampoline to spring ourselves into a significant economic, social, political pinnacle, I think that's a positive," the Governor said. The city finds itself in a position similar to Dallas' in the aftermath of a different tragedy—the assassination of President John F. Kennedy. Dallas was able to transform its image into one of a world-class city, Oklahoma leaders say.

A big part of the local get-out-the-message effort now consists of a $320 million downtown redevelopment package, which includes the new ballpark and other projects. But the tragedy keeps a grip on the public's emotions, because Oklahoma City is a big small town where seemingly everybody knows somebody affected by the explosion.

The process of recovery and renewal looks ahead to the eventual construction of a national memorial on the Murrah site and a nearby museum. The site remains an attraction reminiscent of Dallas' former Texas School Book Depository and grassy knoll. Quiet visitors come to the Murrah site every day, many attaching mementos and remembrances to the fence that surrounds it. Survivors who return to the site for ceremonies don't seek to keep the tragedy in the public eye for any personal gain, Dr. Heath said. "This is not a story about Paul Heath who was in the Murrah Building at the time of the bombing," he said. "This is a story of a young man Timothy McVeigh whose delusional political thinking was so out of line and so extreme that he was driven by a desire to start a revolution. This was an attempt to dismantle the kind of constitutional government that we have. The story is bigger than us as survivors. And so when we continue to keep this story alive, we're keeping the story alive long enough to get the memorial built in order to extend our collective memory of this evil event… by memorializing the good that came out of it."

Reprinted with permission of the *Dallas Morning News.*

"Focus Moves to Programs; Admission Prices Unchanged," by Jack Money, *The Daily Oklahoman,* August 17, 2001

With 230,000 paid admissions into the Oklahoma City National Memorial Center in its first six months of operation, even the most skeptical would agree the memorial has arrived.

The memorial staff's mission will shift gears as the center enters its first full fiscal year of operation Oct. 1, members of the trust overseeing the memorial were told Thursday. Continued development of educational and outreach programs will replace memorial construction as priorities. The staff also must begin to think of maintenance issues for the center and outside memorial to victims of the Oklahoma City bombing. These details and others were reviewed by members of the Oklahoma City National Trust as they approved an operational plan and financial budget for the coming year. The budget detailed how revenues from paid admissions into the museum will pay for the memorial's operational expenses. Many of those expenses are being paid today by the Oklahoma City National Memorial Foundation while the trust finishes paying for construction of the memorial center. "Going through this process of putting together a budget is kind of scary for us right now," said Kari Watkins, executive director of the memorial center. "But by this time next year, we expect we will be a lot smarter about how we think our annual revenues and expenses will do in the coming year."

The budget approved by the National Trust Thursday projects that 384,000 people will visit the memorial center between Oct. 1 and Sept. 30, 2002. Those visitors are expected to generate $2.45 million in revenue from ticket sales and $768,000 in gift shop sales. Admission to the memorial center costs $7 for adults, $6 for adults older than 62, $5 for children with student identification cards, and nothing for children ages five and younger. The fees will not be changed in the coming year. After taking out the costs for the gift items, the trust expects to make about $2.9 million in the fiscal year. Operational expenses are projected to run $16,000 over that. Plans call for the deficit to be made up with interest proceeds from an endowment fund under the memorial foundation's control. "But we don't want to tap into that money if we don't have to," Watkins said. "And if we make more than we plan, then whatever is surplus will go to the foundation for investment." The operational plan approved by the trust refines the roles of Oklahoma City National Trust and National Park Service employees for the memorial.

The Oklahoma City National Memorial is unique because—unlike most national monuments and parks—it isn't owned by the federal government. Instead, the land and space inside the Journal Record Building for the memorial center are owned by the trust, which includes local stakeholders. The National Park Service is paid for the services provided by eight local rangers to the museum site. Mary Bomar, Oklahoma's National Park Service coordinator, said the process of creating the operational plan for the memorial was a good one for all concerned. "We have learned an awful lot about each other and our cultures, as well as our vision for the future," Bomar told the trust. "The process was difficult at times, but it also was rewarding as we opened up…and generated creative ideas that challenged us to stretch beyond the boundaries of normal problem solving." Linda Lambert, who chairs the trust, also talked Thursday about a just-started process to create a five-year strategic plan for the memorial. Lambert said she hoped a group of volunteers making up numerous committees and the memorial's staff would complete work by mid-November. "What are our new goals and priorities? This is pretty ambitious, but folks also said we couldn't build a memorial in six years," Lambert said.

Reprinted with permission of *The Daily Oklahoman.*

san francisco

1 Harry Bridges Plaza HERB LINGL

2 Protestors meet to fight construction of the Embarcadero Freeway in San Francisco SAN FRANCISCO CHRONICLE

1/4 MILE

TO MARINA DISTRICT

SAN FRANCISCO BAY

TELEGRAPH
HILL

LOMBARD

COLUMBUS

NORTH
BEACH

THE EMBARCADERO

CHINATOWN

NOB HILL

FINANCIAL
DISTRICT

UNION
SQUARE

MARKET STREET

SOUTH
BEACH

ENDERLOIN

SOUTH OF
MARKET

MISSION STREET

INTERSTATE HIGHWAY

san francisco

Like many urban areas around the United States, the San Francisco Bay Area has been in a slow process of recovery from the highway building of the 1950s and 60s and de-industrialization. By 1980, the ROMA Design Group, an interdisciplinary San Francisco-based urban improvement firm, had already put forth a plan to remove the Embarcadero Freeway, which, built in 1956 had cut off the downtown area of the city from the waterfront for close to thirty years. So while the devastation caused by the Loma Prieta Earthquake in October 1989 was a cause for great pain for the city, it also brought about one of the most remarkable processes of American civic improvement of the past decade. Willie L. Brown, the mayor of San Francisco, commented about the freeway removal: "We talked about it, but we would never have torn the elevated freeway down—we couldn't get the political muscle. After the earthquake, we had a golden opportunity, and we didn't know how awful that elevated freeway was until it was removed. Harry Bridges Plaza is a legitimate major public space, and may very well be the pioneer public space for San Francisco." Beyond the removal of the freeway in 1992, the city of San Francisco also committed itself to the redevelopment of the entire Embarcadero waterfront into public open space. Harry Bridges Plaza reestablished the civic character of the Embarcadero waterfront and the restoration and expansion of the one hundred-year-old Ferry Building into a modern ferry terminal and farmers' market has transformed the area into a "working" waterfront for public use. The earthquake, ironically became a turning point for Bay Area urbanism.

Aerial view of San Francisco with Pacific Bell Park on left, South Beach Marina in center and Harry Bridges Plaza on upper far right HERB LINGL

73 SAN FRANCISCO | TIMELINE

3

timeline> 1906

APRIL 18 The Great Earthquake strikes San Francisco at 5:13 a.m. and is felt from Coos Bay, Oregon, to Los Angeles, and as far east as central Nevada, an area of about 375,000 square miles. The Earthquake causes the Great Fire, which continues to burn for four days. The death toll is estimated at more than 3,000 and damage is approximately $500,000,000 in 1906 dollars.

1915

FEBRUARY 20 San Francisco hosts the Panama Pacific International Exposition to celebrate San Francisco's rebirth after the 1906 earthquake and fire.

1956

Embarcadero Freeway is built from the Bay Bridge and around downtown to Broadway Street, despite public protest in one of the first freeway fights in the nation.

4

5

Completion of the freeway all the way to Golden Gate Bridge, however, is halted upon citizen protest. **2** **4**

1962

A $20 million bond provides for renovation of the Civic Auditorium that houses the Panama Pacific Organ, built for the Panama Pacific International Exposition in 1915 and since fallen into disrepair.

1980-88

The Northeastern Waterfront Plan is prepared by ROMA Design Group, an interdisciplinary practice of architects, landscape architects and urban planners based in San Francisco, working with three City agencies (the Planning Department, the Port and the Redevelopment Agency), a 32-member Citizens' Advisory Committee and the local community. The plan sets forth a new vision for the waterfront and the redevelopment of underutilized and vacant lands for a major new residential neighborhood centered on parks, promenades and a recreational marina, and

> **"The changes on San Francisco's northern waterfront show how careful planning can turn perils—an earthquake, the port's demise—into opportunity. It can also be so defensive that the built environment offers nothing to rival the magnetism of the natural one."**
>
> **John King,** Urban Design Writer,
> *San Francisco Chronicle*

a mixture of office and commercial uses. The plan calls for the removal of the Embarcadero Freeway and the improvement of The Embarcadero as a recreational and transit-oriented boulevard. **6**

1983 ROMA Design Group is selected by the Port of San Francisco and the Recreation and Park Department to design Pier 7, an 800-foot recreational and public access pier on the downtown waterfront.

JULY State of California Department of Transportation proposes I-280 Transfer Concept Program to use federal freeway construction funds for non-freeway alternatives, including the removal of the Embarcadero Freeway. Traffic planning is undertaken and alternative plans are developed for the redesign and improvement of the Embarcadero roadway.

1985 Approximately $5 million in public funds are received from the State and the City for the construction of Pier 7.

1988 Construction begins on Pier 7.

Northeastern Waterfront Advisory Comittee discussing the master plan for San Francisco 1979 ROMA DESIGN GROUP

6

Mayor Willie L. Brown with a model of the Mid-Embarcadero Transportation and Open Spaces Project ROMA DESIGN GROUP

7

1989

OCTOBER 17, 5:04 p.m. The Loma Prieta Earthquake with a Richter magnitude of 7.1 strikes the San Francisco Bay Area killing 62 people, injuring 3,700 others and displacing approximately 12,000. The earthquake is centered about 60 miles south of San Francisco, and is felt as far away as San Diego and western Nevada. Many of the double-decker highways throughout the Bay region are damaged. Over 20,000 buildings are damaged, 18,000 of which are homes. Damage and business interruption estimates reach $10 billion; $2 billion is for San Francisco alone. President George H. W. Bush declares a disaster area for the seven hardest-hit counties, from Monterey and San Benito in the south to Marin and Solano in the north.

Subsequently, Caltrans (California Department of Transportation) evaluates the Embarcadero Freeway and determines that it is not cost effective to repair the existing structure.

1990-93

1990 A Committee for a Safe Embarcadero is formed, advocating demolition of the freeway.

Pier 7 is completed. **9**

1990-1993 A series of public presentations and meetings about the future of the Embarcadero Freeway takes place.

APRIL 18 San Francisco Board of Supervisors and Mayor Frank Jordan endorse the concept of a surface or subsurface replacement project on the Embarcadero.

JULY 30 Embarcadero Freeway Demolition and Replacement Report is presented to the San Francisco Board of Supervisors.

OCTOBER 1991 A report with the Central Embarcadero Urban Design and Transportation Recommendations is produced, emphasizing the use of the city grid for traffic distribution as an alternative to freeway replacement.

8

FEBRUARY 12 Environmental Assessment: US Department Of Transportation and the Federal Health Administration issue Finding of No Significant Impact (FONSI) for the Embarcadero Surface Roadway Project.

1992 The California Department of Transportation demolishes the Embarcadero Freeway. 5

APRIL 27, 1993 ROMA Design Group presents Freeway Replacement Options to the Public Utilities Commission and Mayor Frank Jordan.

1994

Port of San Francisco embarks upon a feasibility study to restore the Ferry Building.

FEBRUARY-JUNE Stakeholder/Community Workshops are held about the future of the Ferry Building and its role within a redeveloped waterfront.

Port of San Francisco and ROMA Design Group embark upon a preliminary design for the Downtown Ferry Terminal.

"Our main concern was how to make Harry Bridges Plaza a lively, open place where people felt comfortable during the day and at night. We began to rethink the grid and how we could integrate the boulevard with six lanes of traffic but maintain a public space where the vehicular traffic didn't dominate the pedestrians."

Bonnie Fisher,
Principal, ROMA Design Group

1996

NOVEMBER 4 San Francisco Bay Conservation and Development Commission (BCDC) recommend ROMA's roadway alignment and urban design concept for the Embarcadero project.

San Francisco Board of Supervisors endorses ROMA Design Group's "Mid-Embarcadero Transportation and Open Spaces Project," which covers an area of one-and-a-half miles of the San Francisco downtown waterfront. The project in summary:

- Plaza. A new one-acre plaza extending from the Cityside Park to the Ferry Building. Improvements include tree planting, landscaping, new lighting, and other amenities. Two "light cannons" will shoot beams of light 600 feet into the sky. 7

- Cityside Park. A newly designed park with a Music Pavilion on the south to house the Panama Pacific Organ.

- Ferry Terminals. Two ferry basins will be introduced to accommodate expanded ferry travel.

- Historic Trolleys. The F-line along the entire waterfront will be completed running historic trolleys. A new transit stop will be built within the plaza enabling the trolleys to extend all the way down Market Street to Fisherman's Wharf.

- Ferry Building. Interior and exterior renovation of the Ferry Building will be undertaken by San Francisco-based architects SMWM. (The Ferry Building, built in 1898, and designed by architect Arthur Page Brown, was once second only to Charing Cross Station in London as the busiest transit terminal in the world.) SMWM proposes to restore the building's 660-foot-long nave and extend it to the first level, creating a public galleria running the length of the building, and renovate the second floor passenger gallery. A portion of the building will become a market hall on weekends and will open out to include the Ferry Plaza Farmers' Market, which established itself on the Mid-Embarcadero immediately after the removal of the freeway. The two upper floors will be developed as office space. ⓫

DECEMBER An Environmental Assessment (National Environmental Policy Act) and Initial Study (California Environmental Quality Act) is drafted for the Mid-Embarcadero Transportation and Open Spaces Project.

1997-98

FEBRUARY The San Francisco Bay Conservation and Development Commission (BCDC) approves refined concept for the Mid-Embarcadero.

AUGUST 8 San Francisco Planning Department and The San Francisco Port Commission adopt ROMA's plan for the Mid-Embarcadero.

SEPTEMBER 22 San Francisco Board of Supervisors and Mayor Frank Jordan adopt the Final Urban Design Treatment for the Mid-Embarcadero Roadway.

JUNE San Francisco Board of Supervisors approves design of the Music Concourse in Cityside Park.

JULY Construction begins on Mid-Embarcadero Transportation and Open Spaces Project.

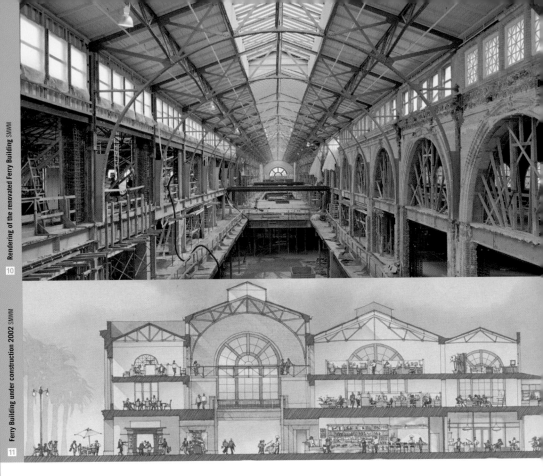

2000-04

APRIL 2003 Ferry Building is scheduled to reopen.

2004 Music Concourse is scheduled to be completed.

FEBRUARY 2000 Construction starts on North and South Ferry Terminals.

JUNE 16 Mid-Embarcadero Transportation and Open Spaces Project is dedicated. Embarcadero Plaza is renamed Harry Bridges Plaza. 1 8 3

JUNE 24 Mayor Willie L. Brown hosts a media tour with U.S. Secretary of Transportation Rodney Slater.

AUGUST Governor Gray Davis approves appropriation of funds for the project.

JANUARY 2001 Construction starts on Ferry Building and East Promenade. 10

JULY Annual *San Francisco Chronicle* Marathon passes through Embarcadero Plaza.

OCTOBER 3 South Ferry Terminal opens.

DECEMBER 2002 East Promenade is scheduled to open.

Mid-Embarcadero Transportation and Open Spaces Project
CLIENTS: Port of San Francisco, State of California Department of Public Works, State of California Department of Transportation, State of California Department of Parks and Recreation, City and County of San Francisco
URBAN DESIGNERS AND ARCHITECTS: ROMA Design Group, in association with the San Francisco Department of Public Works

Ferry Building
CLIENT: Port of San Francisco
DESIGNERS: SMWM
HISTORIC PRESERVATION: Page & Turnbull
RETAIL ARCHITECT: Baldauf Catton and Von Eckartsberg
STRUCTURAL ENGINEER: Rutherford & Chekene
DEVELOPER: Wilson/Equity Office and Wilson Meany
PROPERTY MANAGER: Primus Industries

Waterfront Pavilion
CLIENT: Waterfront Pavilion Committee, Friends of Recreation and Parks, San Francisco Department of Recreation and Parks, City and County of San Francisco
ARCHITECTS: ROMA Design Group

Pier 7
CLIENT: Port of San Francisco and SF Recreation and Park Department
ARCHITECTS: ROMA Design Group
STRUCTURAL ENGINEER: TY Lin International

Downtown Ferry Terminal
CLIENT: Port of San Francisco
ARCHITECTS: ROMA Design Group
COASTAL ENGINEERS: Moffatt and Nichol

san francisco's waterfront

JOHN KING in conversation with
RAYMOND W. GASTIL

John King is the Urban Design Writer for the *San Francisco Chronicle*. In 2002 he was a finalist in the Criticism category for the Pulitzer Prize and in September 2002, he received a Presidential Commendation from the California chapter of the American Institute of Architects for bringing public exposure to design issues.

Raymond W. Gastil: In the 1950s, the visual connection between the main axis of downtown San Francisco, Market Street, and the turn-of-the-century Ferry Terminal Building on the northern waterfront was cut off by a double-decker highway. In the 1989 earthquake, that highway was so damaged that it had to be torn down, and for the first time in 40 years, the city was reconnected to its waterfront, far more than in the 1970s Embarcadero Center projects, which were still screened off by that elevated road. Did San Francisco turn a disaster into an opportunity? What was the urban design process and result?

John King: At that site, there are four different pieces of public space: Justin Herman Plaza, between the end of Market Street and the former highway; another piece where the ramps came down on the same side, one piece immediately in front of the Ferry Terminal Building, and then the area roughly where the road was, where Harry Bridges Plaza is now. When it came time to do that plaza, at the center of these spaces, it would have been the logical time to think about it all as a single entity.

But you had complicated ownership patterns, and you had a political desire to get things finished as promptly as possible. One of the pieces, where the highway's ramps came down, would have been a logical in-fill development site, possibly for a large open farmers' market. There had been a very successful waterfront farmer's market for a few years after the elevated roadway came down, at the foot of the ferry building, and it looked like a permanent one with a food hall could go in this space. Civic activists in the apartment buildings directly to the north argued to keep that as green space, and the Board of Supervisors ended up saying "that is a park." So you're left with this odd green area that doesn't really fit in with anything. Close to this is the Vaillancourt Fountain, pretty much the most despised fountain in San Francisco and designed to have a freeway running behind it. You go in the back, and it's a hideous wall of stained concrete. There was talk of dismantling it, but it is public art, and there was fear this

might trigger legal delays. The new space, after the highway came down, was at the foot of the ferry building, where ROMA's original plan was to create a grand plaza, with the light rail curved along the edge, and with the six lanes of traffic alongside. Many good planners objected that this would be an unsafe asphalt barrier. So the final design is this teardrop, a large, landscaped median. The final product works in a functional way, but I've never heard anyone say, "Hey, let's go to Harry Bridges Plaza, I'll meet you down there, and then we'll walk to the ballgame." Given the initial decisions not to play with the spaces a bit, I don't know if you could have done anything different. It works more as a piece of the city, rather than the heart and soul, except for New Years and other special events when they close the whole thing off, when it does become the classic urban public space.

RWG Is the best public space in cities about special events, everyday events, or just a place to cross through? How does this section of the waterfront work in those terms?

JK That's the challenge of urban place, how do you respond to the city around you, and this part of the city is so in flux. A more uniform space that had a sweep to it, and also lots of activity jutting into it, could have become the place where the east side of the city would want to go for lunch.

RWG Will that change when the ferry terminal reopens as a mixed-use center?

JK During rush hour you have real paths of foot traffic from the ferry, but at 11:00 a.m., it will depend on if the ferry building has office workers and shops and other things that create a casual back and forth. And if the hotel planned on the south edge along Mission Street gets built, and the hotel has a good edge to it, you'll start to see people coming from different directions at different times.

RWG Does this waterfront work for public transportation and pedestrians?

JK Yes, but not as well as it could. You cannot catch the trolley at PacBell Park and go to Fisherman's Wharf—the system south of the Ferry Building ties into the city's central subway, while the northern route is a continuation of a vintage trolley route that runs on Market Street. Each line had been in the works before the earthquake; they should have been integrated somehow afterwards, but they weren't. Still, each line is great fun—and helpful—on its own.

As for pedestrians, one of the great urban experiences in San Francisco is that when you come out of a game at the end of the night, you can walk up the Embarcadero. It's an intoxicating experience, and one that exists wholly because of that freeway coming down; you can see the smartness of designing it as a grand boulevard and the esplanade on the waterfront itself.

Two things I think were done really well: the palm trees work to create this good strong line on the land signaling what's going on, and then also, even though the transit system doesn't all fit together, nonetheless, the transit lines are good at marking the urban edge as well. You're walking up the Embarcadero after a game taking your time, the train goes by and it's packed with people who are in more of a hurry, and so it feels very urban.

RWG **What does it really take to do an exceptional new place or new district? What are the most important anchors so far besides taking down the highway?**

JK The most important anchor, which really has been a catalyst in the public's embrace of the southern Embarcadero, is the ballpark. A month after the earthquake, there was an election about whether to let a stadium go forward on the site, and it failed very narrowly. It came back when Willie Brown became mayor, and passed by a two-thirds vote. It required no public financing for the actual building, although public money went into preparing the site. Diehard opponents who fought it in the 80s were saying ballparks really screw up the places around them; then in the 1996 election, they said, no—if you do this, it's going to gentrify this area. At the other end of this waterfront, Pier 45 works well as a part of the wholesale fishing industry, but also for small boats. All along the northern edge, the Port owns all the waterfront, and had planned to do incredibly lucrative things. They faced real constraints, from regulations from the Bay Conservation and Development Commission, which did not allow housing or even non-maritime offices on the waterfront. There was a waterfront moratorium on development that lasted six or seven years until a waterfront plan was in place, following a referendum.

The plan was done in 1997, and the smart thing about it is that it allowed the Port to look at the entire waterfront, so it could then sit down with the state regulatory commission, the BCDC, and other groups and kind of do horse-trading. You know, "give us development options up here, and let us do fairly free development on these piers, and in return, we'll tear down those piers," rather than each pier being an all or nothing kind of thing. Five years later, nothing has been built on Port land, yet, though a lot of projects are in discussion. With everything that gets done in San Francisco, certainly everything on the waterfront—each interest group has its 100% view of the world.

RWG **Would you conclude that San Francisco seized the moment?**

JK Yes. The earthquake shattered the psychic map for two years as well as the physical one. In some ways I think we're definitely a better city for it. In terms of the waterfront, there was a realization that if ever there was an opportunity to undo our mistake, this is it, and it was done. San Francisco took the opportunity to say we need to see this marvelous place as a marvelous place, and look at it in unity.

1 Workers rebuild the roof of the National Library (1997) FERHAD MULABEGOVIC

2 Aerial view of Sarajevo ELIE DERMAN

sarajevo

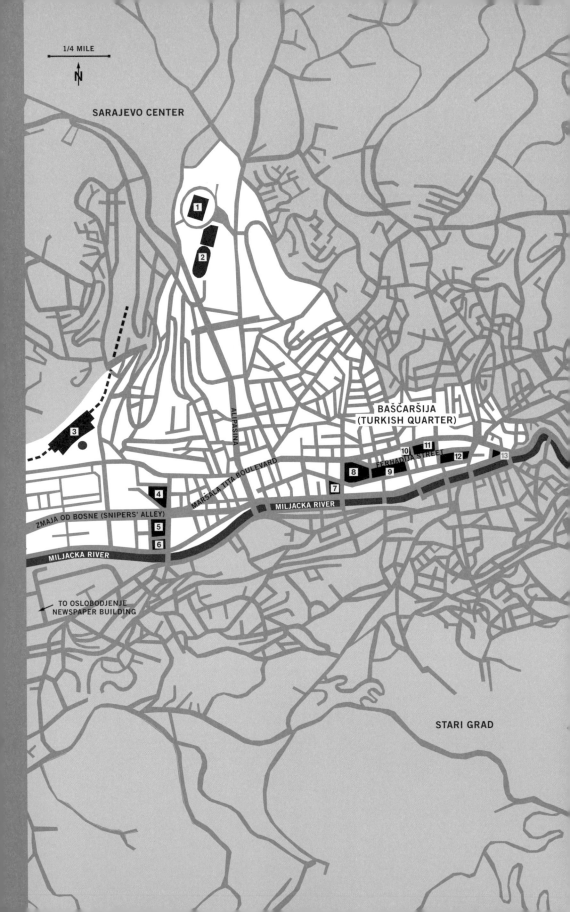

sarajevo

Since the three-year siege on Sarajevo ended in 1993, the city has steadily been renovating the national landmarks destroyed in the war. Zetra Ice Stadium, designed by architects Dusan Dapa and Ludimil Alikalfic in 1984, and used as a morgue during the siege, was the first such landmark to be restored to its former glory in 1999. The following year, the Sarajevo Main Post Office, designed by architect Josip Vancas and built in 1913, opened after a five-year renovation. And although setbacks caused by lack of funding have meant slow progress, the National Library designed by Alexander Wittek and Ćiril Iveković and built between 1892 and 1896, and formerly the Town Hall, has entered its second phase. Perhaps of greatest loss to the capital city, which has a population of over half a million and is situated on the Adriatic, was the destruction of the library and its archives, which have erased almost all the records of the history of Bosnia-Herzegovina, leaving it in a state of historical amnesia. Ferhad Mulabegovic, the architect entrusted with its restoration, explains that the "National Library ranks among the greatest and the most representative buildings of the Austro-Hungarian period in Bosnia-Herzegovina. The building has become a symbol of Bosnia-Herzegovina."

With the reopening of each landmark, Sarajevo gets closer to returning to the status it enjoyed during the Winter Olympics of 1984. However, this city is still far from full recovery. The three years spent under the siege of the Bosnian Serb army not only destroyed the physical infrastructure of the city but also shook the foundations of the life of its inhabitants. Parks were turned into cemeteries, and the former cosmopolitanism of the city has suffered at the hands of fundamentalist organizations and hard-line nationalists. However, the city is overcoming these hardships — it has structured the Sarajevo Bidding Committee to try to win the Winter Olympics for 2010 and has organized, for the eighth successful year, the Sarajevo Film Festival.

Aerial photograph of Sarajevo taken before the siege began in 1991 MOMIR HRISAFOVIC, FROM THE TEXT URBICIDE BY SRDJA HRISAFOVIC

timeline> 1984

WINTER Sarajevo hosts the Winter Olympic Games in the new Zetra Ice Stadium designed by architects Dusan Dapa and Ludimil Alikalfic. 2 3

1992

MARCH Bosnia-Herzegovina declares independence from the former Yugoslav Federation.
The Serbs living in this ethnically diverse region fear control by the Muslim Slav majority. Fighting breaks out between the factions. The majority of towns fall to Serb control, with the exception of Sarajevo, the capital city of the Republic of Bosnia and Herzegovina.

APRIL 5 The Yugoslav National Army attacks Sarajevo.

MAY 2 The "Siege on Sarajevo" begins.

The Zetra Ice Stadium is destroyed.

SARAJEVO

I WANT YOU TO SAVE SARAJEVO
NEAREST RECRUITING STATION

LET THE GAME START NOW!

WAKE UP EUROPE!

SARAJEVO '94

SARAJEVO CALLS EVERY MAN WOMAN & CHILD

The Main Post Office building, as well as a 1959 annex and the post terminal are destroyed by detonations. 6 7

AUGUST The Vijecnica Town Hall, which houses the National and University Library, containing Sarajevo and Bosnia's historical public records and national archives, is shelled with incendiary munitions. More than 70% of the library holdings are lost. The steel dome above the central hall is severely damaged. Despite the seemingly intact façade, the interior is completely destroyed.

The largest commercial buildings in Sarajevo, the Unis Towers, at the eastern end of Snipers' Alley, designed by architect Ivan Straus, are severely damaged by shelling.

1993

Artists and designers respond to the seige. 4 Trio Design Sarajevo, founded by Bojan Halilovic and Dalida Durakovic, produces a series of handmade postcards entitled "Greetings From Sarajevo." The ironic postcards are redesigns of well-known

advertising and Pop Art images such as Coca-Cola, Absolut Vodka and Your Country Needs You. The postcards carrying messages about the war in Sarajevo are displayed all over Bosnia and internationally within newspapers and magazines. 5

JULY Acclaimed writer and director Susan Sontag travels to the city to stage Samuel Beckett's play "Waiting for Godot" with Serbian and Bosnian actors.

1995

OCTOBER 25-NOVEMBER 5 The first Sarajevo Film Festival is held in the besieged city. 37 films from 15 countries are presented at the Bosnian Cultural Center. The Festival draws more than 15,000 viewers, resulting in sold-out performances every night.

DECEMBER With the signing of the Dayton Peace Agreement approaching, Implementation Force (IFOR) planners identify Zetra Ice Stadium as a location for occupation by the ACE Rapid Reaction Corps when United Nations Protection Force (UNPROFOR) transfers authority to IFOR. Hundreds of personnel take up residence in what becomes known as Ice Station Zetra.

A structural renovation project, headed by DOM Consulting, Designing and Engineering Shareholding Company of Sarajevo, begins on the Main Post Office. In addition, over the next five years, a major interior renovation takes place led by Sarajevo-based architects Ferhad Mulabegovic and Mustafa Gutic.

1995-1998 Inspections of the National Library are undertaken to determine the extent of the damage to the building. Renovation plans are designed by Ferhad Mulabegovic based upon his findings. 10 11

1996

The Austrian government donates approximately $1 million for the renovation of the National Library. Total damage to the National Library is estimated at more than $10 million.

> **"The National Library housed within the Town Hall in Sarajevo, and built in 1896, ranks among the greatest and the most representative buildings of the Austro Hungarian period in Bosnia-Herzegovina. Its renovation was very important. The building has become a symbol of Bosnia-Herzegovina and is presented in Sarajevo's picture postcards."**
>
> Ferhad Mulabegovic, architect.

FEBRUARY 26 Sarajevo is proclaimed an open city. The northwest passage is opened and the districts of Vogosca and Ilijas are liberated. By the time the siege ends government reports estimate that 10,615 people are dead and more than 50,000 are injured. Estimated damage costs to the city's buildings and infrastructure exceed $13 billion.

SEPTEMBER 9 Rudolf Thiel, an architect by profession and the force behind the prestigious Berlin meet, organizes a special track and field meet to take place in the damaged Kosovo Stadium in an attempt to bring normality back to the war-torn capital.

1996-1997 The first phase of renovation of the National Library begins. Fallen and unstable materials are removed and the attic structure is reconstructed according to the original architectural drawings. The steel dome and glass roof covering the central hall are repaired. Steel scaffolding is built around the central staircase to prevent further damage, and in anticipation of the second phase of renovations. 1 12

National Library KIMBERLAE SAUL

1997

APRIL 3 Pope John Paul II holds a Catholic mass at Kosovo Stadium.

SEPTEMBER 23 Billed as the biggest concert ever staged in Sarajevo, the Irish rock group U2 holds a concert at Kosovo Stadium. This is the first event of its kind to be held in the city since the siege began.

Local government authorities and the Olympic Committee of Sarajevo asks that the SFOR (Stabilization Forces) vacate the Zetra Ice Stadium on the grounds that they had obtained funding to rebuild it. SFOR vacates the stadium and restoration work begins.

The Austrian government pledges $825,000 to replace the roof of the National Library.

1998-99

Technical support documentation for the second phase of the renovation of the National Library is prepared. The European Commission is expected to donate nearly $2 million for the project.

"In 1993, during U2's Zooropa tour, the group had a live satellite link-up to people in Sarajevo to show what was happening there during the siege. Bono made a promise to the Bosnian people that he would bring the next U2 tour to Sarajevo. He kept the promise, and in 1997 while things in Sarajevo were still not 100% stable he went there. This was the first positive thing that had happened in Sarajevo since the siege began. It was a chance to show the world through the media that it was time to go back and rebuild the city."

Andraz Brzin, photographer

1999 The $22 million reconstruction of the Zetra Ice Stadium, the majority of which was donated by the International Olympic Committee, is complete.

MARCH 30 NATO bombers attack Yugoslavia, Bosnia's neighbor to the east. Airports in the region are closed. The reopening ceremony for the Zetra Ice Stadium is cancelled.

MAY 28 The Zetra Ice Stadium is reopened.

JULY Balkan Summit Meetings are held at the Zetra Ice Stadium.

National Library before renovation FERHAD MULABEGOVIC

National Library under construction FERHAD MULABEGOVIC

NOVEMBER 22 Urban Future Organisation, a London-based international team of design professionals, is announced the winner of a year-long international design competition for the Sarajevo National Concert Hall. Located in the heart of the city, the National Concert Hall will be integrated into the surrounding site to create an anchor for one of Sarajevo's most important public spaces. It is designed to accommodate a large concert hall, as well as small performance spaces, meeting rooms, a library, restaurant and bookstore. **13 14 15**

20,000 people who fled Sarajevo during the siege return.

2000

International sporting groups and private companies pour millions of dollars into rebuilding some of Sarajevo's winter sports facilities.

The Trade Development Agency's (TDA) Railways Recovery Rehabilitation Project gives $660,000 towards the reconstruction of Bosnian railways.

TDA's Olympics Site Hotel Feasibility Study provides a $256,000 grant to the canton of Sarajevo for a feasibility study for a hotel and conference center on a site adjacent to the Zetra Ice and Kosovo Stadium.

TDA's Sarajevo Corridor Intermodal Terminal Study awards a $450,000 grant for partial funding of a feasibility study for intermodal container facilities between the Port of Ploce, a Croatian port to be leased to the Bosnian government under the terms of the Dayton Peace Agreeement, and Sarajevo.

2001

SPRING Construction begins on the Sarajevo National Concert Hall.

MAY 3 Inauguration of the reconstructed Main Post Office. "The Post Office has remained firmly in the memory of the citizens of Sarajevo. In addition to its main purpose as a post office, it can be used as a space for art exhibitions and theatrical performances. Since it has been renovated it has also become a cultural center." Ferhad Mulabegovic, architect. **8**

SEPTEMBER 4 The non-governmental and non-profit organization Garden of the Righteous is founded with the intention of establishing a Garden of the Righteous in Sarajevo, which will commemorate the most recent human sufferings from warfare in Europe. The garden will include: "A memorial to all those who opposed the killing, abuse, and humiliation of innocent people. The United Humanitarian Mission (UHM), a nonprofit organization from San Francisco, offers Sarajevo a universal monument to the Righteous, with the goal of commemorating those whose experience could be transmitted to future generations for their education. The monument will be in the form of a museum, built on the site of the garden and will serve as an extensive research center for studying ethics and ethical behavior. UHM plans to offer to build the same monument in all countries in which genocide has occurred in the twentieth century."

2002

SPRING Second phase of National Library renovation begins.

2008

Scheduled completion date of the Sarajevo National Concert Hall.

National Post Office
CLIENT: National Post Office
ARCHITECT: DOM Consulting, Designing and Engineering Shareholding Company of Sarajevo with Ferhad Mulabegovic and Mustafa Gutic
STRUCTURAL ENGINEER: Edhem Kapidžić
ELECTRICAL ENGINEER: ELMAHING, Sarajevo
MECHANICAL ENGINEER: CLIMA TRADE

Vijecnica Town Hall, National Library
CLIENT: Vijecnica Town Hall, National Library
ARCHITECTS OF THE ORIGINAL BUILDING: Alexander Wittek and Ćiril Iveković
ARCHITECT OF RENEWAL: Ferhad Mulabegovic
CIVIL ENGINEER: Edhem Kapidžic, Taib Hadžovic, Omer Ćaušević, Dr. Zlatko Langof and Dr. Muhamed Zlater

Sarajevo National Concert Hall
CLIENT: EU Commission/Comune di Roma - Zone Attive
ARCHITECT: Urban Future Organisation
CONSULTANTS: AKTE Engineers, BDSP Partnership, Davis Langdon & Everest, Carr & Anjier, Halcrow Fox, Sandy Brown Associates

landmark reconstruction

FERHAD MULABEGOVIC in conversation with JON CALAME

Ferhad Mulabegovic is a Bosnian architect who has had a leading role in the conservation of architectural icons throughout Sarajevo. Jon Calame is a founding partner and Operations Officer of Minerva Partners, Inc., a New York-based consultancy for heritage conservation. He is currently co-editing *No Man's Land: The Spatial Anatomy of Five Divided Cities,* with Esther Charlesworth, to be released in summer 2003.

Jon Calame: Can you describe the context for your recent work in Sarajevo and the challenges facing the country in the course of postwar physical reconstruction?

Ferhad Mulabegovic: After the Dayton Peace Agreement was signed, Bosnia-Herzegovina faced the challenge of establishing priorities for its recovery. The country, which had become poor, accepted donations from numerous countries, from multinational entities like the United Nations and the European Union, from private foundations and donors, etc. Initially, Bosnia-Herzegovina proceeded with reconstruction of housing, returning the population to their homes, reconstruction of schools, hospitals and infrastructure as well as revitalization of the cultural and historic heritage.

As well as being the capital of Bosnia-Herzegovina, Sarajevo is the largest university center, the headquarters of the State Government, and the Government of the Federation of Bosnia-Herzegovina. It is the city that is being reconstructed and revitalized most intensively. Bosnia-Herzegovina is a country in transition, a country that has not yet passed all the relevant laws related to physical reconstruction and planning. This is a country with no money to activate its economic assets and start up industrial production. It is a country with a very high unemployment rate, around 40%. Bosnia-Herzegovina is becoming increasingly a country of the young and old, lacking the most productive middle-aged population that was displaced during the war. It will take a number of years to establish a new economic system enabling the country to exist independently of foreign donors and their agencies. According to the Dayton Peace Agreement, Bosnia-Herzegovina was divided into two Entities, the Federation of Bosnia-Herzegovina and Republika Srpska, each of which consists of ten cantons. It will take time to establish harmonious relationships between all these entities and parties.

JC The transition you mention from dependency on foreign donor agencies to national industry is a difficult and important one, especially for large-scale infrastructure and urban reconstruction programs. How prepared are politicians and professionals in Bosnia-Herzegovina to fundraise and manage major physical projects after the foreign donor agencies pull out?

FM Since the end of the war, foreign donors have financed the reconstruction of Bosnia-Herzegovina through their agencies. Bosnia-Herzegovina is a small but complex state, which must be responsible for the key investments in capital infrastructure projects (lines of communications, energy projects, etc). At the same time, the Entities, in realizing the common interest of the country, should try to act in compliance with the state institutions.

JC Do strategies and timetables exist for the transition of Bosnia-Herzegovina from recipient (of foreign donations for reconstruction) to investor?

FM In this post-war period, the State itself cannot act as an investor since it has not yet activated its production. The high unemployment rate speaks clearly to the problem of a State that still cannot realize its own profits in order to invest independently in large public projects. It will take more time until we are able to do this ourselves.

JC How do you think Bosnia-Herzegovina will achieve sustainable development for historic sites in the next ten years?

FM With change of ownership in the historic centers, with new investment from individuals, the country will soon accelerate the development and infrastructural upgrade of historical centers. Changes are visible already: the historical center of Sarajevo was significantly rehabilitated after the war's destruction, and recovery is visible in the reconstruction of the historical center of Mostar. For other historical places, it is necessary to pass rehabilitation plans, to reach out to new investors, to accept tourism as a serious economic generator, and to incorporate all these elements into the reconstruction of historical centers like Pocitelj, Stolac, and Travnik.

JC What is the value of physical reconstruction of architectural landmarks with respect to reconciliation and social development in Sarajevo?

FM Before the war, both Bosnia-Herzegovina and Sarajevo were proud of their multi-ethnic and multi-religious character. Mosques and churches were built next to each other, and people were tolerant. It is hoped that this traditional value will regain importance after architectural landmarks are reconstructed.

Sarajevo, built under Turkish rule, developed fully during the Austro-Hungarian period and became a new city. Following World War II, it succeeded in defining its development through strong programs that protected its historic heritage. Destruction of the city and its architecture during 1992-1995 and the establishment of new economic relations after the disintegration of the Communist government caused problems that have not yet been brought under control and as a consequence great problems continue to arise. One of the greatest problems is construction without building permits that cannot be monitored or halted. Politicians, instead of the institutions in charge of planning, are still making decisions related to urban development. However, it is expected that the expert institutions will assume a key role after the necessary laws have been passed.

JC Can you be more specific about which laws should be adopted to manage cultural heritage outside a central governmental framework, and based on which models?

FM Here the generally accepted attitude is that it is necessary to pass laws on cultural management for the whole state of Bosnia-Herzegovina, and not only at the city or canton levels, as is the case now. In December 1999 UNESCO offered a law for the protection of cultural heritage at the federal level. This law was not adopted. In the meantime, during the last three years, several partial laws have been passed but they do not correspond well to the overall interest of the country. UNESCO will have to offer a set of revised suggestions.

JC So the process of urban planning and reconstruction is so far heavily shaped by the same kinds of partisan politics that contributed to the conflict in the first place. In your view, what are the impacts of this politicized urban planning?

FM Over the past 50 years politics has played a significant role in urban planning. It is expected that politics will continue to influence the overall strategy of urban planning and investment in reconstruction. In these processes, the urban institutes and architects will be called upon to realize all schemes for planning and construction.

JC Given the political nature of urban planning at this time, what is the most appropriate role for planners and architects in the ongoing reconstruction process? Have they been fulfilling this potential in your opinion?

FM In the pre-war period, there were numerous corporations dealing with planning, designing and building in both Sarajevo and Bosnia-Herzegovina. All were state-owned. Today, these institutions do not exist or have become private companies. There are many private design offices in Sarajevo. There are a number of examples of establishing private ateliers along these lines in the Republic of Slovenia and Croatia. In these places, such private ateliers are treated as equal entities with government offices.

JC It is true that privatization of planning and reconstruction processes previously monopolized by the State is essential. Given this, how can market-driven, private sector initiatives for urban planning and cultural heritage protection be coordinated to avoid redundancy and reflect national priorities?

FM In the first place, the following should be said: Bosnia-Herzegovina as a single country must have a strategy of physical planning for the whole country, as it had before the war. This central framework provides freedom for local planning at the city or cantonal level, and also allows for the inclusion of private sector initiatives.

JC What kinds of assistance is currently supporting the physical reconstruction work, and how is the broader architectural rehabilitation program in sync with social programs, educational, political reform, and economic transition?

FM The rehabilitation is being developed with international assistance. The cultural and historic heritage is a part of the memory of the inhabitants, and at the same time an important component of the process of social reconciliation. International foundations and organizations are reconstructing their own buildings others are being financed with the resources of Bosnian corporations. These include office buildings from the Austro-Hungarian period, including the Bosnia-Herzegovina Post Office. The reconstruction of infrastructure is being financed by the Government of Bosnia-Herzegovina and assorted donor countries. During 1997-2002, the Swedish Foundation for Cultural Heritage without Borders rehabilitated several important cultural monuments in Bosnia-Herzegovina. These included the National Museum and the Despic House in Sarajevo.

JC What about professional partnerships?

FM Many donors have participated in the rehabilitation of buildings of cultural and historic importance through the institutions for protection or in direct cooperation with the owners of the buildings, including the European Commission.

JC You have been deeply involved in several of these projects. Can you explain more about how the remaining funds will be found? How were the previous donations acquired? What are the primary obstacles for attracting support to physical reconstruction?

FM In 1996, the Austrian Government donated $1 million to restoring the National Library. The European Commission provided $2 million for the reconstruction works carried out in 2000 and will support those to be performed in 2002. However, $10-12 million is needed to fully restore the building. There may be new international donors, but in my opinion we are not yet ready—even ten years after the war—to make key decisions about a new function for the old building. As author of the rehabilitation project, I can say that no further step-by-step investment is possible without making clear decisions concerning the building's future owners, users, functions and all other accompanying logistical issues.

JC You mention that the decisions about the library's use, function, and owner are not yet made; who will make these decisions and how?

FM After work on the second phase of the reconstruction begins in October 2002, and in light of discussions on the occasion of the tenth anniversary of its destruction–25 August 2002–it is expected that the canton and city authorities and the ultimate beneficiary, the National and University Library, will define a single multi-functional program.

JC Bosnia-Herzegovina is the ideal example of a multicultural built environment. Its political and cultural history is defined by mixing/being subjugated...and therefore ongoing hybridization and assimilation. This makes it very poignant and beautiful, and lately contested. As the large political blocs of the Cold War dissolved, old national myths and identities—long dormant—resurfaced as ethnic communities sought identity and protection in their chaotic environments. Because so many groups cohabitated in Bosnia-Herzegovina for so long, the built environment was found to "contradict" the chauvinist sermons of the post-war political entrepreneurs, leading to the purposeful destruction of architectural objects that did not fit the script, along with libraries, archives, institutions, etc. It is an excellent case study of violent, reductive irredentism that comes in the wake of major political shifts.

afterword ZOË RYAN

Information Exchange: How Cities Renew, Rebuild, and Remember, forms both a catalogue to the exhibit "Renewing, Rebuilding, Remembering" and is a special edition of our ongoing series of *Van Alen Reports.* Given the rich content of the exhibit and the positive local and international media response, the Institute decided to produce a special edition of the *Report* to document and expand on the exhibit. In addition, this publication emphasizes our continued effort to furthering the exchange of ideas about architecture, planning and design and fostering an informed dialogue on cities.

Exploring how a diverse range of cities have renewed their urban life after manmade and natural disasters, the exhibition places the events of September 11 within a global historical and cultural context and demonstrates that there is not only room but also a necessity for creative solutions to rebuilding cities. Immediately after September 11, an intensive period of research ensued as we brainstormed about the type of exhibition that would reflect multiple responses to disaster. An extensive call for ideas resulted in enthusiastic correspondence with architects, designers, planners, policy makers, artists and members of the general public around the world, who were interested in taking part in the project and impressed that New Yorkers were looking to learn from the experiences of the rest of the world.

Within a month the Institute selected seven cities. As well as wanting to show how cities had recovered from a range of disasters, a criterion for their inclusion was how relevant they were to New York: what lessons could be applied? For instance, questions relating to how New York can better disseminate information on the rebuilding of Lower Manhattan resonate in the project for an Info-Box in Berlin; Oklahoma City National Memorial figures as the precedent for how to organize and run a competition for a memorial in an urban environment; and the role of temporary art in urban renewal is demonstrated through Beirut's "Archaic Procession" public art project.

During the three months that followed, the Institute reached out to hundreds of people who generously donated photographs, contacts and articles. It was inspiring to watch information pour into the Institute. Together with a team of dedicated researchers, we extracted the main projects from each city and developed a timeline outlining the processes of redevelopment, illustrated by hundreds of images. We emphasized photography as our medium in order to engender an immediate response. At the same time that people were doing speculative work about the future of Ground Zero, our research was a valuable counterpart and received much interest from high school students, university design studio groups, city agencies, design firms and the general public. The gallery also became the venue for scores of volunteer meetings about the future of Lower Manhattan.

With our exceptionally committed designers Thomas de Monchaux and Donald Shillingburg, who worked under incredible time pressure, we devised an organizational system for the exhibition, carried forward throughout the design. Whether following the linear order of the exhibition's timelines or cross cutting from one city to the next, visitors are able to draw immediate connections between the processes of urban renewal. The inspired exhibit design is made from plywood and scaffolding, generously donated in New York by Atlantic-Heydt Corporation whose crew took time off from working at Ground Zero to install the pipe columns and I-beams of a sidewalk bridge. The images are pasted like posters to the plywood in a black and yellow color scheme (with printing kindly donated by National Reprographics, Inc.), deliberately recalling construction sites and street maintenance and alluding to the complex conditions of the World Trade center site.

The exhibition is divided into four sections, beginning with a wall of historical images of the cities before disaster, accompanied by city maps with key sites highlighted. Seven "Information Booths" pasted with images post-disaster and timelines explain the process of reconstruction and development, the role of the key players, and significant art and architectural projects. Cutouts in the booths at eye-level allow views of the historical photographs from one side and from the other visitors catch glimpses of the seven 10-foot high images of new buildings, which are hung on the adjacent wall. At the end of the exhibit a reading room with continually updated information about the World Trade Center site in the form of plans, reports, maps, and photographs connects the visitor to New York.

Together with the international press coverage, we are thrilled that the value and message of the exhibition will carry on when it is shown at Glasgow's design center, The Lighthouse, on the initiative of its director, Dr. Stuart MacDonald, from January 25 to March 14, 2003, where Belfast will be added, and where it will inform an international conference on cities. Plans are underway to show it at additional venues internationally.

For their insightful comments, amenability and commitment to the project we would like to thank the interviewees, essayists and reporters featured in this catalogue; as well as Sue Hale from The Daily Oklahoman and Lois Reed from The Dallas Morning News. We would like to especially acknowledge the Institute's Trustees for their belief in this exhibition and subsequent publication, made possible by the Van Alen Institute Trustees Fund. Thanks also to the numerous people—listed at the end of this catalogue—who generously contributed photographs and information to the catalogue and exhibition; to Hello for their exceptional graphic design work on this publication, and in particular Connie Koch and Cindy Heller for their bold approach and hard work; to Sara Moss for her perseverance and dynamic map designs featured at the beginning of each chapter; to Michael Osman for additional research for the catalogue; and to Distributed Art Publishers for supporting this project.

renewing rebuilding remembering

VAN ALEN INSTITUTE, NEW YORK
February 12-July 9, 2002

THE LIGHTHOUSE, GLASGOW
January 25-March 14, 2003

EXHIBITION CURATORS
Raymond W. Gastil
Zoë Ryan

EXHIBITION ADVISORS
Mildred Friedman
Marc Tsurumaki
Nathaniel H. Brooks
Claire R. Nelson

EXHIBITION DESIGNERS
Thomas de Monchaux
Donald Shillingburg

RESEARCHERS
Abby Bussel
Yoshiko Sato, Morris Sato Studio
Kimberlae Saul

FURTHER RESEARCH
Julie Behrens
Jena MacDonald
Marion Poessl
Marcus Woollen

EXHIBITION INSTALLATION
Jeremy Linzee
Dan Berry
Steve Caputo
Ayesha Menon
Sasha Nicholas
Ron DeVilla
Phillip McKinley

SPONSORS
National Reprographics, Inc.
Atlantic-Heydt Corporation
Van Alen Institute Trustees Fund

SPECIAL THANKS TO:
The Irwin S. Chanin School of Architecture
of the Cooper Union; Columbia University
Graduate School of Architecture, Planning,
and Preservation; Nicholas De Monchaux;
Evan Douglis; Michael S. Fishman;
Paul Lewis; Edward T. Linenthal; Miko McGinty;
The New York Times; Phil Nutley;
Elizabeth O'Donnell; Max Protetch Gallery;
James S. Russell; Susi Sánchez

BEIRUT
Mahfoud N. Aji
Corinna Dean
Makram el-Kadi
Kathryn Gustafson, Gustafson Porter, Ltd. (USA/UK)
Angus Gavin, SOLIDERE
Nadim Karam
Bernard Khoury Architects
Layth Madi
Klaus Würschinger

BERLIN
Schneider + Schumacher Architekten
Eisenman Architects
DaimlerChrysler
Atelier Dreiseitl
Jörg Hempel
Sara Moss
Renzo Piano Building Workshop
Lara Swimmer

KOBE
Shigeru Ban Architects
Shuji Fujita, CITY of KOBE
Haruo Hayashi, Research Center for Disaster Reduction Systems
Nobuaki Ishimaru, ARXKOBE
Kazuto Kasahara, Kyoto Institute of Technology
Tomoko Kawayoshi, Nojima Fault Museum
Yoshihiro Matsuda, Showa Sekkei Architects, Planners & Engineers
Katushiro Miyamoto, Atelier Cinquième Architects
Kazuhiro Miyata, *The Kobe Newspaper*

MANCHESTER
Hodder Associates
Manchester City Council
Nic Clews
EDAW
Architecture Foundation
Len Grant
Hemisphere
Euan Kellie
Aidan O'Rourke

OKLAHOMA CITY
City of Oklahoma City Planning Department
Joshua Gelfman
Ross Barney + Jankowski, Inc.
Anthony L. Lindsey
Oklahoma City National Memorial
Butzer Design Partnership

SAN FRANCISCO
ROMA Design Group
Willie L. Brown, Mayor, City and County of San Francisco
John King, Urban Design Writer, *San Francisco Chronicle*
SMWM

SARAJEVO
Andraz Brzin
Mark Burrell
National Olympic Committee, Bosnia-Herzegovina
Elie Derman
Momir Hrisafovic
Srdja Hrisafovic
Miroslav Kraijtmajer
Ariel Krasnow
Ferhad Mulabegovic
Urban Future Organisation
Endi Poskovic
Trio Design Sarajevo